MW01408696

JAPANESE EXPORT CERAMICS 1860-1920

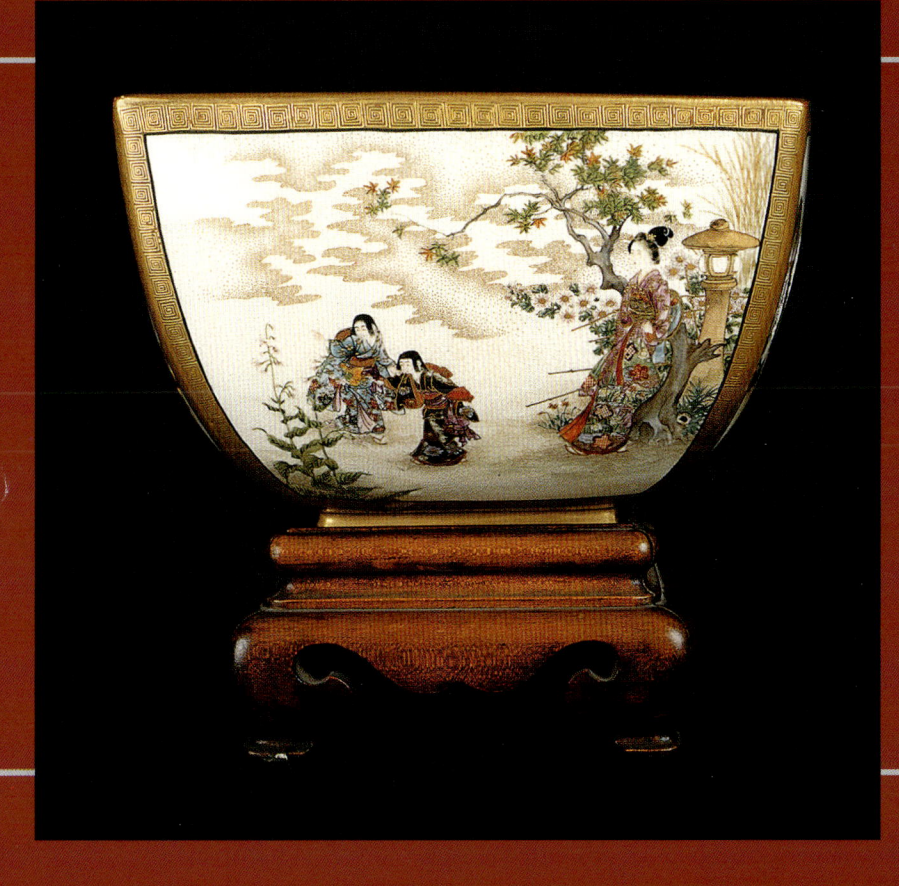

Nancy N. Schiffer

Schiffer Publishing Ltd
4880 Lower Valley Road, Atglen, PA 19310 USA

Library of Congress Cataloging-in-Publication Data

Schiffer, Nancy.
    Japanese export ceramics, 1860-1920/Nancy N. Schiffer.
       p. cm.
    Includes bibliographical references and index.
    ISBN 0-7643-1043-7 (hardcover)
    1. Porcelain, Japanese--1868- 2. Pottery, Japanese--1868- I. Title.
    NK4567.6.S35 2000
    738'.0952'09034--dc21   99-053649

Copyright © 2000 by Nancy N. Schiffer

All rights reserved. No part of this work may be reproduced or used in any form or by any means—graphic, electronic, or mechanical, including photocopying or information storage and retrieval systems—without written permission from the copyright holder.
"Schiffer," "Schiffer Publishing Ltd. & Design," and the "Design of pen and inkwell" are registered trademarks of Schiffer Publishing Ltd.

Cover design by Bruce Waters
Book designed by Blair Loughrey

Type set in Caxton Lt Bt/Zurich/Korinna
ISBN: 0-7643-1043-7

Printed in China
1 2 3 4

Published by Schiffer Publishing Ltd.
4880 Lower Valley Road
Atglen, PA 19310
Phone: (610) 593-1777; Fax: (610) 593-2002
E-mail: Schifferbk@aol.com
Please visit our web site catalog at
www.schifferbooks.com
Please write for a free catalog.
This book may be purchased from the publisher.
Please include $3.95 for shipping.

In Europe, Schiffer books are distributed by
Bushwood Books
6 Marksbury Ave.
Kew Gardens
Surrey TW9 4JF England
Phone: 44 (0)208-392-8585; Fax: 44 (0)208-392-9876
E-mail: Bushwd@aol.com
Free postage in the UK. Europe: air mail at cost.
Please try your bookstore first.

We are interested in hearing from authors with book ideas on related subjects.

CONTENTS

ACKNOWLEDGEMENTS 4
SHAPES AND DECORATIONS 5
EXPORT TRADE IN
   JAPANESE CERAMICS 6
IMARI PORCELAIN 14
   Figures of Women 15
   Figures of Men and Boys 25
   Animals 29
   Plates, Round 31
   Plates, Shaped 38
   Bowls 44
   Bottles 48
   Vases, Floral 52
      People 59
      Birds 62
      Dragons 63
      Fish 64
   Jars and Garniture 66
   Specialty Shapes 71
HIRADO PORCELAIN 73
   Figures 73
   Plates, Round 78
   Plates, Shaped 80
   Bowls 81
   Bottles 81
   Vases 82
   Jars 84
   Specialty Shapes 86

KUTANI PORCELAIN 88
   Figures 89
   Plates, Round 92
   Plates, Shaped 93
   Bottles 94
   Vases 96
   Jars 106
SATSUMA EARTHENWARE 107
   Figures of Women 108
   Figures of Men and Boys 113
   Animals 116
   Plates, Round 116
   Plates, Shaped 119
   Bowls 120
   Bottles 124
   Vases, Floral 127
      People 134
      Birds and Animals 162
   Jars 167
   Specialty Shapes 170
   Decorators of Satsuma............... 177
   Kinkozan 177
   Makuzu Kozan 191
   Ryozan 194
   Seikozan 196
   Yabu Meizan 200
BIBLIOGRAPHY 205
INDEX 206

ACKNOWLEDGMENTS

Kevin Page and Christopher Page of Kevin Page Oriental Art in London caught our enthusiasm for this book project and consented to our photographing their vast collection to demonstrate the shapes and decorations in so many variations. The study took on its own life as the connections between the pieces emerged through comparisons and contrasts. As additional collections were studied, more similarities emerged as well as shapes and designs not seen before. We thank the following people for their generous sharing of knowledge, study pieces, and hospitality:

Marvin Baer of Ivory Tower Antiques, Ridgewood, New Jersey;
Drick-Messing Collection;
Akira Fukagawa, Iwao Fukagawa, and Yutaka Hashiyama of the Fukagawa Porcelain Manufacturing Company in Arita, Japan;
Meyers-Voll Collection;
W. Parker;
Tom and Linda Tompkins;
Bruce Waters.

Together, you have added immeasurably to the merging picture of export ceramics as ever-evolving trade goods that continue to decorate and fascinate the Western world.

And I am indebted to photographers Bruce Waters and Blair Loughrey for so cleverly capturing the images so we all may continue the study.

The ceramics shown in this book are courtesy of an anonymous private collection and of Kevin Page Oriental Art, Camden Passage, London, except as otherwise noted.

SHAPES AND DECORATIONS

The Japanese export ceramics in the following study are arranged for present-day consumers who generally consider items first by their shapes, and then by their decorations. Therefore, the different styles of ceramics explored here (Imari, Hirado, Kutani, and Satsuma) are further divided by their shapes (plates, bowls, etc.) and then by their ornamental decorations (flowers, animals, architecture, etc.). That is how the market is driven today, and so it should be easy to find the type of ceramic you seek by this organization.

Almost invariably these ceramics are loved for their forms and surface decorations; they are almost exclusively ornamental goods in the Western world. These vases almost never contain flowers. The water jars have never been filled. The incense burners have never produced a whiff of scent. The Western consumers value the decorations above all else and have consistently been willing to pay good money for precise craftsmanship that produces intricate, imaginative, and —above all else— exquisite workmanship. Long lost are the Chinese or Japanese stories that originally may have inspired a design, for they no longer have any relevance to the society into which the pieces are sold. Today collectors have an infatuation for the pretty and intriguing decorations displayed on the surface and the interesting shapes of many of the pieces.

EXPORT TRADE IN JAPANESE CERAMICS

Japanese Developments

Western knowledge of Japan began quite by accident. Marco Polo wrote of his fantastic travels in China between 1271 and 1287, including Chinese accounts of "the land of the rising sun," now called Japan. Astute members of the Roman Catholic Church read Polo's books and thought of the fertile potential Japan provided for converts to Christianity, but they did not act on the idea immediately.

Around 1543, shipwrecked Portuguese merchant/sailors Crisobal Baralho, Fernao Mendez Pinto, and Diego Zaimoto were rescued by Chinese pirates and disembarked after a terrible storm on the Japanese island of Tanegashima. Japanese authorities who learned of the intruders sent Pinto to the town of Funai, but he fled to the tiny Portuguese settlement at Macau on the Chinese coast, together with an outlawed Japanese Samurai murderer named Anjiro. By 1545 Pinto was back selling firearms to Japanese anarchists.

At this time there were conflicts among provincial leaders in Japan, and soon Portuguese ships were made welcome on the coast of Kyushu to supply firearms, soon known as "Tanegashima weapons" after their first appearance on that island.

Before too long, Portuguese Jesuit priests accompanied Portuguese traders back to Japan, and the Japanese, noting the respect they received from the Portuguese officers, treated the Jesuits with similar respect. A young and vibrant Jesuit, Francis Xavier, who had, a few years earlier, helped Ignacius Loyola found the Jesuit order, was at Macau. Xavier took little time to see the potential this newly found land mass provided his order, and he sailed for Kagoshima province in southern Kyushu in 1549, accompanied by Jesuit priests Balthasar de Tories and Joan Fernandez, and the Samurai outcast Anjiro. Francis Xavier was respectfully received by the Japanese leader Shimazu and he traveled to Hirado Island, Nagato, and Bungo, where Christian communities soon were established. Xavier reached Miyako, now known as Kyoto, in 1550, where an important center for Christianity was soon established. The foundation for contact between Japan and the West was therefore complete.

A detailed study of the development of relations between Japan and Western governments over the next five

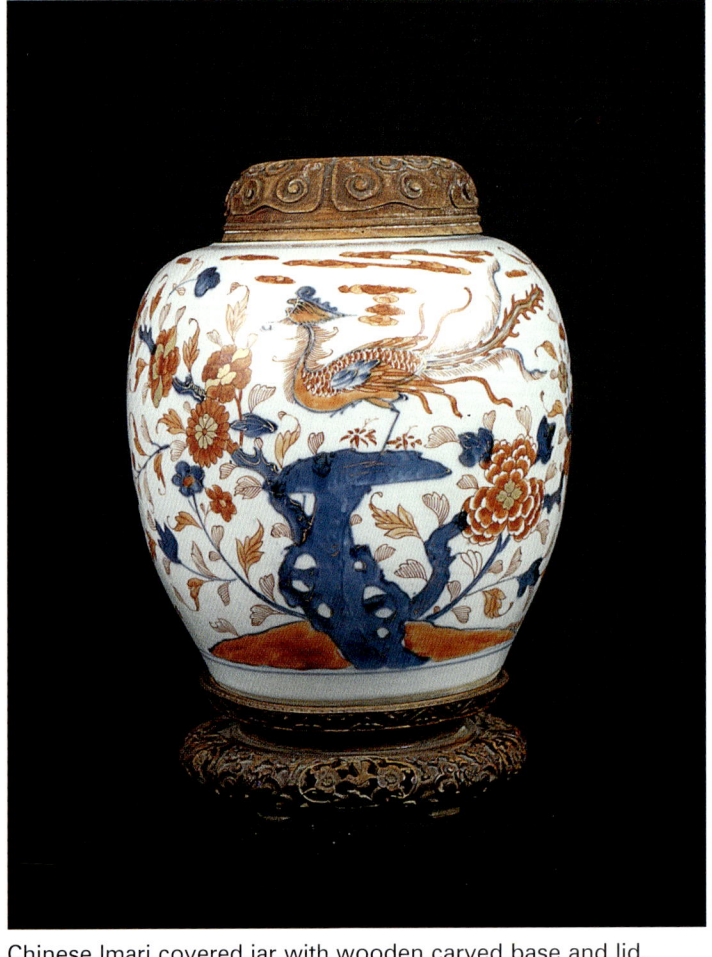

Chinese Imari covered jar with wooden carved base and lid, jar with floral branch, bird, and dragon decoration. Jar 9" h.

~ 6 ~

decades is an intriguing and powerful story. Here we suffice to conclude that trade developed rapidly, as Japanese desired guns and Westerners craved the exotic trade items from both China and Japan. The parties influenced each other profoundly. The Japanese leader Toyotomi Hideyoshi developed a liking of Portuguese dress which he and his retainers occasionally wore by 1594. Christianity was both accepted and rejected by different Japanese parties with passionate zeal. Upon this foundation the trade in Japanese ceramics as export items is based.

All Portuguese missionaries were banished from Japan by 1598, the same year the Japanese leader Hideyoshi died. A period of political strife in Japan extended from 1598 to 1617, during which persecution of Westerners in Japan was exercised in earnest. Dutch trading ships were permitted to come first to tiny Deshima Island in Nagasaki harbor on the southwest coast of Kyushu island in the first quarter of the seventeenth century. When the English pilot William Adams arrived at the harbor of Funai in 1600 on a Dutch ship of trade, he had with him letters from English King James I for the highest Japanese leaders. Another phase in Japanese-Western relations was about to begin.

Ships, first from the Dutch East India Company, (founded 1602) and later from the English East India Company (founded 1715), were granted trade privileges in Japan. The companies dealt with representatives of the new leader, Tokugawa Ieyasu, who began the Tokugawa dynasty which has become known as the Edo Period (1615-1868). William Adams became an advisor to Tokugawa on military and naval matters, especially as they concerned Western nations. The Dutch hold on trade with Japan waned as the English increased their Naval supremacy and subsequent influence in Asian trade.

During this same period, within the first two decades of the seventeenth century, porcelain clay was found in the

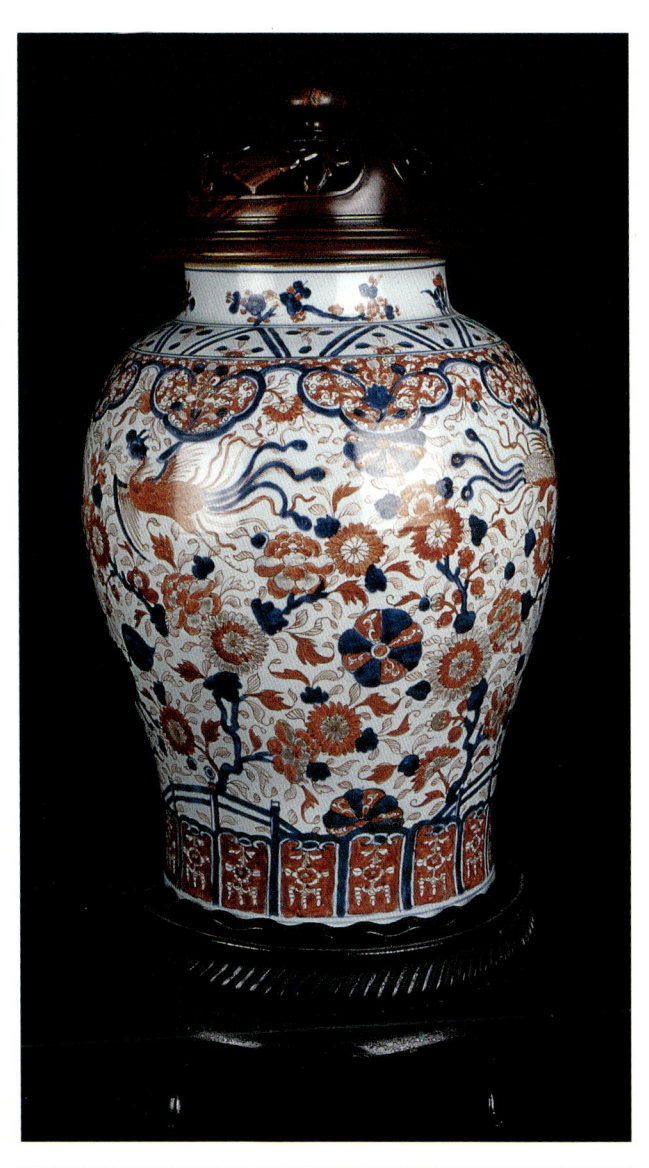

Large Chinese vase with wooden lid and ho-ho bird and floral decoration, 18th century. Vase 19.5" h. $6,440

Blue and white round dish of Kraak style with deer and floral decoration, c. 1700, 15.25" d. $2,900

Japanese mountain Izumiyama, near Arita, in the Southwest region of Kyushu by Korean potter Ri Sampei. He had been brought with other potters to Japan in 1597 by Hideyoshi to develop a ceramics industry in Japan. He (they) did, eventually, and the Dutch found a market in Europe almost immediately for Japanese ceramics, no matter how primitive they were at the time. These early Japanese export ceramics influenced European ceramics dramatically (such as Dutch and English Delftware). The Dutch set up a ceramics factory (Vereenigde Oost Indische Compagnie, or V. O. C. for short), first located on Hirado Island, and moved in 1641 to Deshima Island at Nagasaki. Dutch merchants had exported blue and white glazed ceramics similar to Chinese "Kraak porcelain," and Chinese "Imari" styles which they no longer could obtain in China. From 1653 to 1682, the Dutch depended on the Japanese wares to continue their Western trade. A variety of Japanese ceramics from the 1650-1700 period were shipped to Europe, India and Persia, most of white body with blue underglaze designs.

The potter Sakaida Kakiemon, from the Arita region, first introduced red enamel overglaze decoration in Japan about 1650, and by about 1660 Dutch traders began sending this new style to Holland as

Large Imari covered jar with floral decoration, c. 1700, 35" h. $11,270

Blue and white double gourd bottle, c. 1680, 16.75" h.

Large Imari dish with central decoration of flowers in a vase and bonsai, six rim patterns with landscapes and floral decorations, c. 1700, 24.5" d. $15,000

Imari straight vase with flaring rim, 12" h., mounted on a European ormolu base.

well. European collectors could not get enough of the curious Japanese ware right up to the beginning of the eighteenth century.

Enthusiasm for Japanese tea and trade goods in the seventeenth century in Europe cannot be overstated. Collections of Japanese ceramics were formed by the most wealthy and discriminating level of society, including the Burghley collection in England (inventoried in 1688), Augustus the Strong's collection in Dresden (formed 1698-1722), the Charlottenberg collection in Berlin, and others. So esteemed were the porcelains that they were sometimes mounted with European ormolu bases and handles.

Although the Dutch East India Company charter to trade with Japan did not expire until 1795, Holland's influence during the seventeenth century gradually declined as it receded as a European naval power. The charter was not renewed after expiration.

For 150 years after 1700, Japan maintained a policy of isolation from "barbarain" ideas from the West and stifled most outside communication. The English East India Company conducted only limited trade in ceramics, largely because European ceramics factories were being founded in the eighteenth century to present serious competition with Chinese and Japanese sources. In Europe, the vague remembrance of exotic trade items from Japan made would-be consumers hungry for any news, books, or goods from the East. And so it remained until the West could stand it no more. Political and trade events culminated with repeated attempts by strong British and American governments to establish relations with Japanese leaders. Always they were officially rejected. Finally, in 1853, American Naval Commodore Matthew Perry and his fleet entered the Tokyo harbor. They carried an official letter from American President Millard Fillmore for the Japanese Emperor and instructions from the American State Department to negotiate a trade ageement. That effort, combined with political struggles taking place in Japan at the time, changed the course of Japanese history. Once again, trade with the West became possible, and within a few years new Japanese ceramics were made available for the craving Western markets.

By the mid-1850s, the Industrial Revolution was in full force in the West, enabling larger numbers of Europeans and Americans to benefit from the efficiencies of machine-based industry. More people gradually were able to possess better quality and lower priced consumer goods in general. Into this growing prosperity, which demanded fancier and more decorative goods now called Victorian, Japanese merchants of a new entrepreneurial class saw opportunity. They found they could produce a wide variety of ceramic goods that were more decorative than useful and that sold well in Europe and America.

While the ceramics industries in Japan were not idle for the 150 years of isolation, they were producing goods almost entirely for consumption in their own lands under a very successful system of feudal patronage. When the government and relations with foreign countries changed in the 1850s, free enterprise was initially possible in Japan and many people made a rapid transition to the new system. Therefore, mass production and volumes of export ceramics became available to the West from Japan from about 1860 forward.

Large Imari vase with floral decoration and a garden fence, c. 1700, 22.25" h.

Western Reaction

The Japanese exhibit at the 1862 International Exhibition in London swept European taste into a tailspin from which it is still recovering. So popular and fascinating were the Japanese arts and crafts to the attendees that art circles thereafter have both embraced and rejected Japanese-style aesthetics generation after generation. A passion for the Japanese and oriental styles swept over the West at all levels of society, starting at the very top. "By the 1870s, Japanese art in every form was readily available in the London stores, including Arthur Liberty's." (Mervyn Levy, *Liberty Style*, p. 20) Liberty at his drygoods store selling Japanese textiles to the theater and avantgarde crowd, James McNeil Whistler in art circles, and Oscar Wilde in the literary world in England each led their fields in the passion for Japanese styles.

In America, the passion for Japanese style was fortified by the large Japan exhibit at the 1876 Centennial Exhibition in Philadelphia, where the Japanese display was the most popular exhibit seen by millions of visitors. Much attention was given to the exhibit of ancient porcelain, earthenware, and stoneware exhibited by the Kirutsu Kosho Kaisha Company, an affiliate of the English designer and "art advisor," Christopher Dresser.

Christopher Dresser went to the Centennial Exhibition in Philadelphia in 1876 on his way to visit Japan. While in Philadelphia, he gave a series of lectures promoting his ideas on "Art Industries, Art Museums, and Art Schools" at the Pennsylvania Museum and School of Industrial Art (now Pennsylvania Academy of Fine Arts), which was newly founded. He complained then that the South Kensington Museum (now the Victoria and Albert Museum) in London "had discontinued the practice of purchasing Oriental and Japanese art, which was such great importance to British designers and manufacturers." (Widar Halén, *Christopher Dresser*, p. 40) Dresser's thoughts were embraced immediately by New Yorkers Charles Louis Tiffany and his son Louis Comfort Tiffany who Dresser met during this trip. "Tiffany had launched some popular silver designs in the Japanese style in the early 1870s, and now commissioned Dresser to bring back a substantial collection of all kinds of artifacts from Japan, amounting to several thousand items. They were delivered to Tiffany's by Dresser on his way home in 1877." (Halén. p. 40, 41)

As arranged before the Philadelphia Fair with the Japanese organizers, many of the ceramics shown in the Japanese exhibit were purchased by British collector and curator Sir A. Wollaston Franks and eventually deposited with the South Kensington Museum . Therefore, this institution contains to this day a fascinating study collection of mid-nineteenth century and earlier ceramics from Japan.

Japanese ceramics continued to be shown to welcoming Western audiences at the International Exhibitions in Paris (1878 and 1900), Chicago (1893), St. Louis (1904), and San Francisco (1915). Many individual artists, workshops, and companies formed in the last quarter of the nineteenth century in Japan furnished goods for this trade and showed their goods at these Inetnational Fairs. Many of them succeeded and endured into the twentieth century. The potter Myagawa Kozan and decorators Yabu Meizan and Kinkozan, among others, produced ceramics in this period which are popular among today's collectors.

The Fukagawa Porcelain Manufacturing Company, of Arita, was formed in the last quarter of the nineteenth century on the foundation of a 300-year-old family ceramics tradition. The business expanded in the 1870s to embrace the export market with items marked Koransha (founded 1875) and Sei Ji Kai Sha, the Comopany of Pure Water (1879-1883). In 1895 the Fukagawa Porcelain Manufacturing Company was founded by Chuji Fukagawa. The company's pieces were included in the Paris (1900) and St. Louis (1904) Exhibitions. The company continues to the present, producing both industrial and ornamental ceramics for a world market.

Import companies developed in the West to manage this trade with Japan, such as A. A. Vantine & Co., Inc. in New York and Yokohama which supplied "Oriental goods" from c.1915-1925. With offices at Fifth Avenue and 39th Street in New York, this company is listed in business directories with Irving Raymond as president and treasurer. A 1916 A. A. Vantine Co. catalog shows Imari, Banko and Sumida Japanese ceramics in many useful shapes for the Western market, including plates, tea pots, and ash trays. A rare porcelain sachet pot in Imari decoration bearing the A. A. Vantine logo, now in a private collection, is shown here; it is a fascinating study piece and indicates that new pieces in Imari decoration were selling well in America in the first quarter of the twentieth century. One must wonder if other promotional pieces were made and can be found today for this and other import companies.

The First World War (1914-1918) and a shift in Western taste from Japanese to Chinese art made the demand for the ornate styles of Imari, Hirado, Kutani, and Satsuma ceramic wares gradually decline after 1915.

Unique advertising sachet pot of Imari porcelain decorated with inscriptions relating to a New York importing company, inscribed: "A. A. Vantine & Co., New York Yokohama, Oriental Sachets," c. 1920, 6.5" h., lid missing.

~ 12 ~

― 13 ―

IMARI PORCELAIN

Japanese Imari porcelain was first made in the mid-seventeenth century near Arita on Kyushu Island from clay found in Izumiyama mountain by Korean potters. First, white wares with underglaze blue decoration were made, and are known today as Arita ware. The first Japanese porcelains to be shipped to European markets were carried by ships of the Dutch East India Company about 1660.

Experimentation in porcelain production in the Arita area in the mid-seventeenth century included underglaze blue and overglaze enamels in red, supplemented with green, yellow, black, gold, and silver. Since some of this was shipped from the port of Imari on the north shore of Kyushu, the multi-colored ware became known in the West as Imari.

In the third quarter of the nineteenth century, a revival of Imari decoration was found to sell well as an export ceramic for the Western market. The Victorian European and American style was very compatible with the deep red, blue and gold tones and the all-over pattern harmonized with some of the popular oriental style rugs used in many home interiors. Many companies produced Imari porcelains in Japan and almost none bear any markings.

FIGURES OF WOMEN

Imari figure of a kneeling woman with a dog, blue iridescence in her robes with gold details and hair feathered at her hairline, base plain white, 7.25" h.

~ IMARI ~

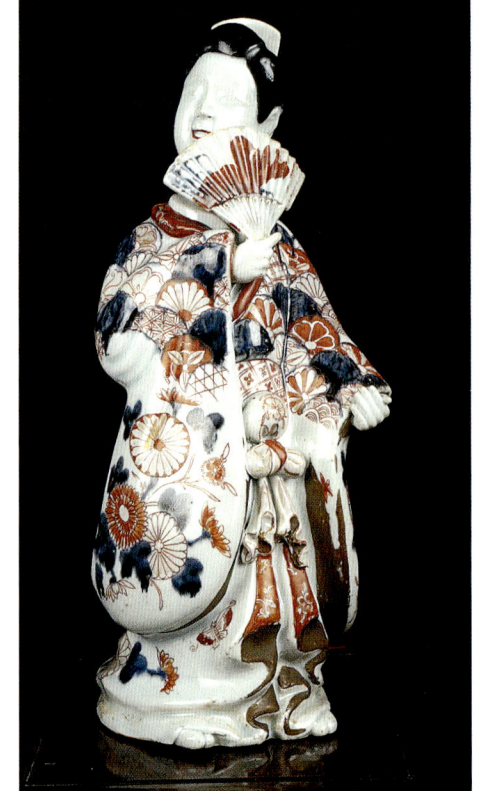

Above: Pair of Imari lady figures, 19th century, very large and unusual Arita ware, 18.5" h. $72,450

Far right: Imari figure of a lady with a fan, c. 1720, 15" h. $4,830-6,440

Right: Pair of Imari figures of courtesans, left hands with detailed fingers and right hands holding a purse, 12" h. $9,660

~ 16 ~

~ IMARI ~

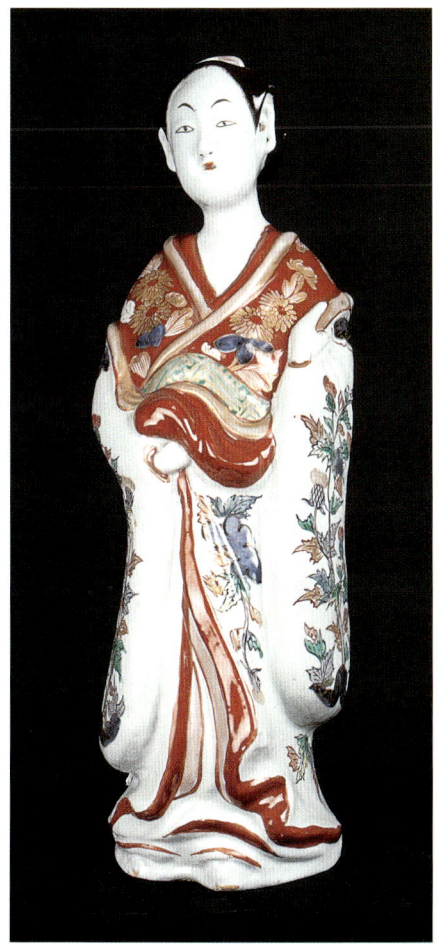

Top left: Single figure of a courtesan standing with crossed arms, 15" h. $4,000

Above: Pair from a set of four matching pairs, of Imari figures of standing courtesans, each holding her skirt, 14" h. Pair $9,660

Left: One of a set of six matching figures of standing courtesans with left hand extended and bent upward, 18.5" h.

~ IMARI ~

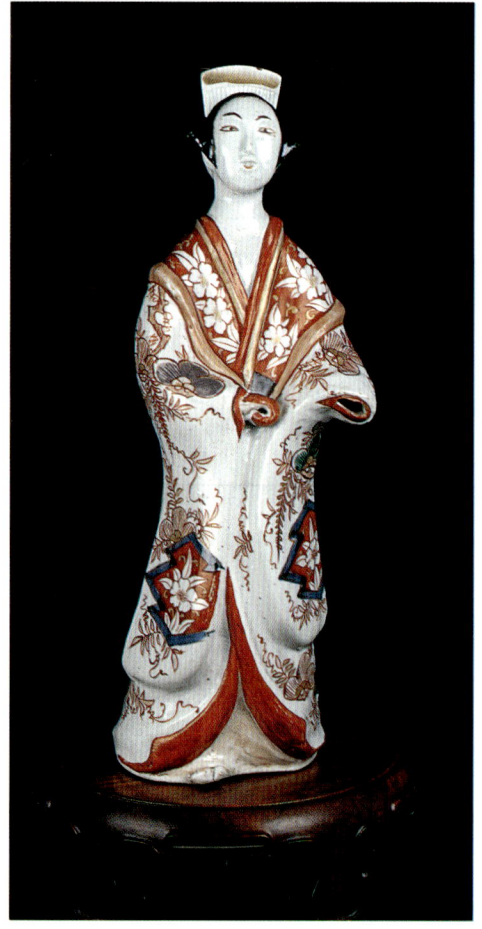

Top left: Pair of Imari figures of standing women in coats, right hand clasping fabric, 12.5" h. (front and back views) $8,855

Above: Single Imari figure of a standing courtesan woman in coat with left hand inside sleeve, 20" h. $5,635-6,440

Left: Single Imari figure of a standing courtesan woman in coat with left hand inside sleeve, 17" h. $6,762-7,245

OPPOSITE
Top: Imari figure of a woman with two baskets, base of bisque with dark brown paint and hair with blue flowers, 12" h.

Bottom: Imari figure of a kneeling woman with iridescent blue glazed robe and gold details, 6.75" h.

~ IMARI ~

~ IMARI ~

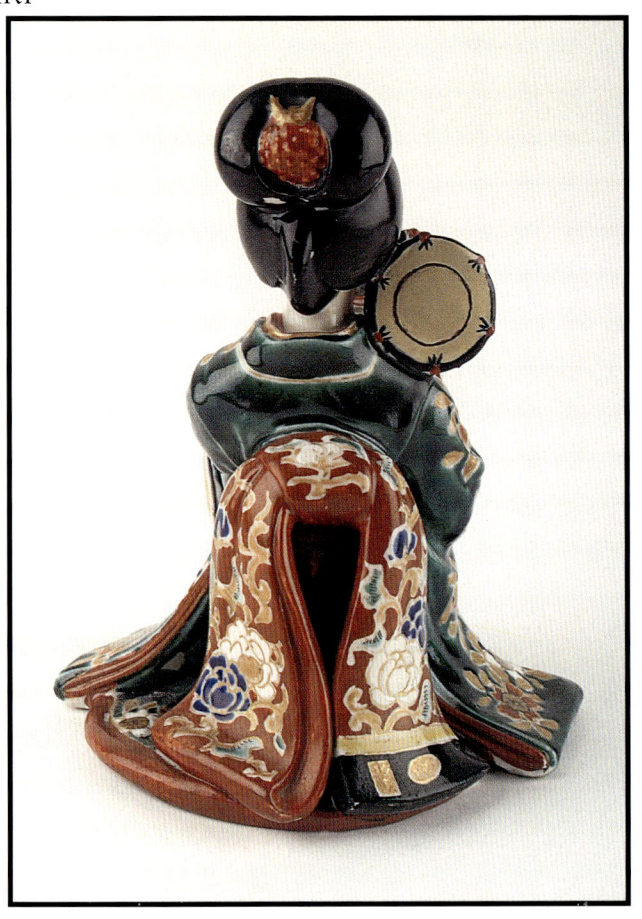

Imari figure of a kneeling lady in green floral robes with two drums, 8" h.

Imari figure of a seated woman in polychrome robes with gold details,
hair feathered at the hairline, white cloth-impressed base, 6.5" h.

~ IMARI ~

Imari figure of a standing woman with blue robes and a dog at her feet, all splendidly painted with great detail including ears exposed in the hair-do, 13.75" h.

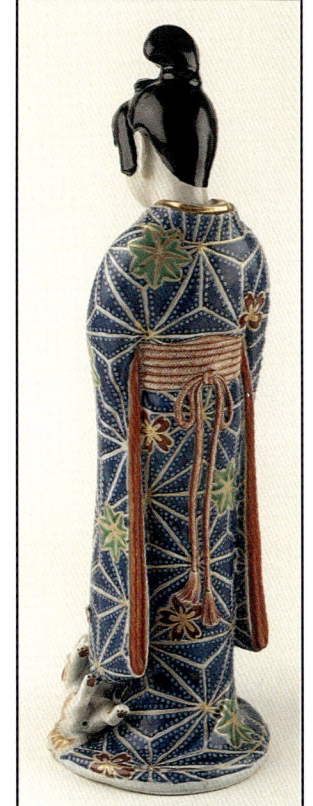

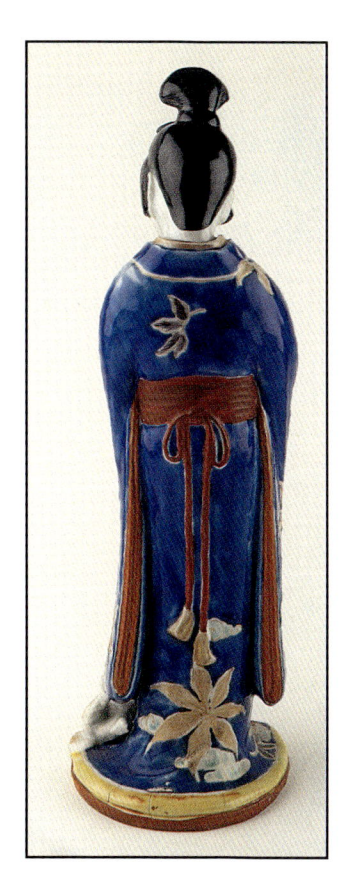

Imari figure of a standing woman with blue robes and a dog at her feet, painting of moderate quality.

~ 21 ~

~ IMARI ~

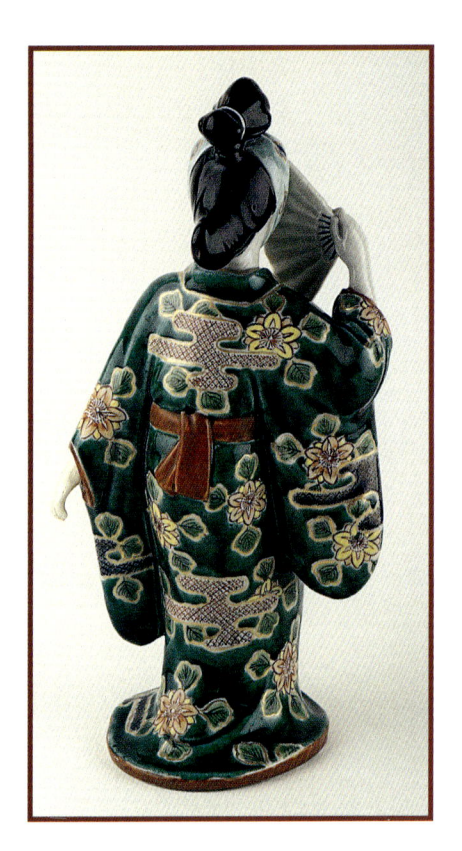

Imari figure of a dancing woman in a green kimono and head scarf with subtle gold decoration with a nicely painted fan, 10.75" h.

Imari figure of a standing woman in a black kimono and white obe holding a closed fan, painted with subtle gold in the decoration, 12.25" h.

IMARI

Imari figure of a woman and a girl standing and holding a cricket cage, beautifully decorated including detailed painting at their hairlines, 14.5" h.

~ IMARI ~

Top: Imari figure of a woman in red robe with a fan, 18.25" h., mounted as a table lamp.

Bottom: Imari figure of a woman in blue robe with a fan, 11.75" h., mounted as a table lamp.

~ 24 ~

IMARI

FIGURES OF MEN AND BOYS

Imari figure of two dancing boys, one with a drum on his shoulder and on with a fan and crane crest. The figure rests on three feet with unglazed bottoms and is ornamented with polychrome decoration, subtle gold details, and finely painted hair, 6.5" h.

~ IMARI ~

Imari figure of a standing boy with a drum and his right arm raised, beautifully painted with details, 9.25" h.

Imari figure of a standing man with a large drum and subtle gold in the decoration, face with subtle painted details, 8.5" h.

~ 26 ~

~ IMARI ~

Top: Imari figure of a standing man with a head band, wide ruffled collar, black skirted robes, and blue floral over-cloak with prominent gold decoration, 12" h.

Bottom: Pair of Imari figures of men in coats, 12.5" h. (front and back views) $8,855

~ IMARI ~

Top: Single Imari figure of a standing man with a fan, white robes with pine and balls design, 18.5" h. $7,245-8,050

Bottom: Pair of Imari figural bookends of seated men in blue floral robes, 7.5" h.

~ IMARI ~

ANIMALS

Above: Imari figure of a lion with raised head and open mouth decorated in blue with red painted floral decoration, 8" h.

Right: Imari figure of a cat with a red collar, floral and gold decorated ruff, and calico markings, 9.5" h.

~ IMARI ~

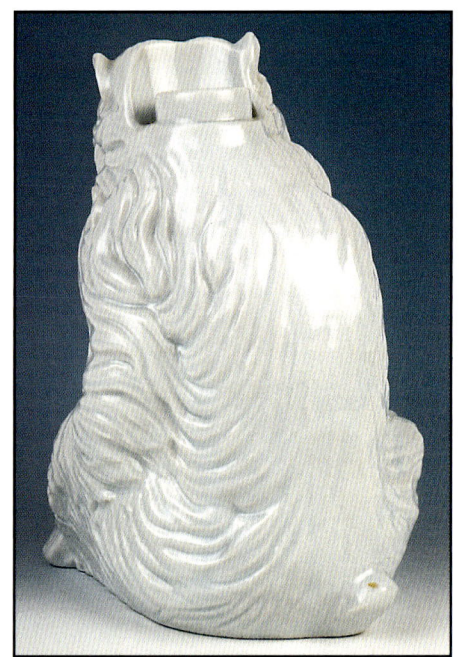

Top: Transitional Hirado/Fukagawa saki pitcher in the form of a seated monkey, 7.75" h. *Collection of W. Parker*

Right: Fukagawa celadon and polychrome glazed bird figurine, 7.75" h. *Collection of Tom & Linda Tompkins*

~ 30 ~

~ IMARI ~

PLATES, ROUND

Pair of large Imari dishes with floral and garden railing central decoration and reserves with flowers in the rim, c. 1870-80, 21.5" d. $11,270

~ IMARI ~

Top left: Imari dish with central landscape decoration, floral sides, and water waves in the rim band, c. 1720, 14.5" d. $2,254

Top right: Large round Imari dish with central ho-ho bird and various patterned rim panels, 24" d. $2,750

Bottom: Large antique round dish with three rounded reserves of bird decoration between three chrysanthemum designs, 21" d. $3,220

~ 32 ~

~ IMARI ~

Top: Large Imari dish with light blue under glaze and orange underglaze decoration, 22.25" d. $1,450

Bottom left: Large round Imari dish with green cranes and dragon, bird, and floral reserves, 20.5" d. $2,254

Bottom right: Large Imari deep bowl painted with a folding screen, 14.5" d. $1,370

~ 33 ~

~ IMARI ~

Round dish with decoration of a folding screen with women in a garden paining, 15.75" d. $1,450

Round dish with fan-shaped reserves of woman seated in a building and ho-ho bird, 15.75" d. $650

Large Imari plate with center decoration of a basket of flowers, and in the rim quail and floral decoration, 18.5" d. $1,130

~ IMARI ~

Deep round Imari dish with floral basket design, 16.75" d. $1,775

Pair of dishes with floral decoration and scalloped rim, 16" d. $1,450

Large round Koransha Imari dish with matte brown background and blue peony decoration, c.1880, 18.5" d. $970

~ IMARI ~

Top left: Koransha large plate with black matte background and blue underglaze blue peony decoration, c. 1880, 18.25" d. $970

Top right: Fukagawa plate with bamboo grove decoration, 15" d. $12,900

Bottom: Large round Koransha Imari plate with landscape group and fan with pine boughs in reserves, c. 1880, 16.25" d. $1290

~ IMARI ~

Fukagawa dish painted with a scene of Mt. Fuji covered in snow, in blue and white porcelain and a rim decoration of gold details, c. 1900-1915.

Fukagawa Imari large plate with red background and cranes in the decoration, 18.25" d. $1,290

Kakiemon style plate with overlgaze bird and floral decoration, 8.25" d. *Collection of Tom & Linda Tompkins*

~ IMARI ~

PLATES, SHAPED

Top: Pair of large scalloped dishes with tapestry decoration, 11.5" d. $885

Bottom: Pair of large Imari plates with scalloped edges and floral decoration in tapestry reserves, 18.75" d. $2415

~ 38 ~

~ IMARI ~

Top: Koransha Imari bowl with central flowers in a vase decoration and floral reserves, c. 1880, 11.75" d. $1,450

Bottom left: Koransha dish with bamboo and plum blossom decoration, c. 1880, 8" d. $400

Bottom right: Koransha Imari bowl with floral decoration and zigzag gold rim, c. 1880, 11.5" d. $1,450

~ IMARI ~

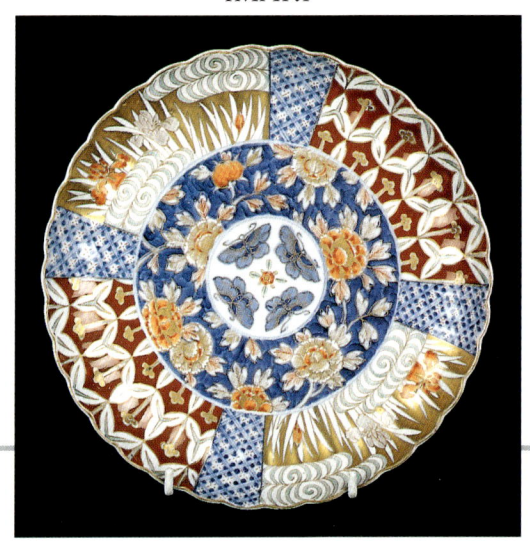

Top: Fukagawa Imari dish with panels of floral and butterfly decoration, 8.5" d. $130

Center: Pair of oval Imari platters with pierced rim and ho-ho bird decoration, 14.5" w. $1,530

Bottom: Oval dish with cut-in edge and two reserves with water scenes, 16" w. $800

~ 40 ~

~ IMARI ~

Imari cake plate with cut-out handles and painted floral and scrolls decoration, 12.75" w. $485

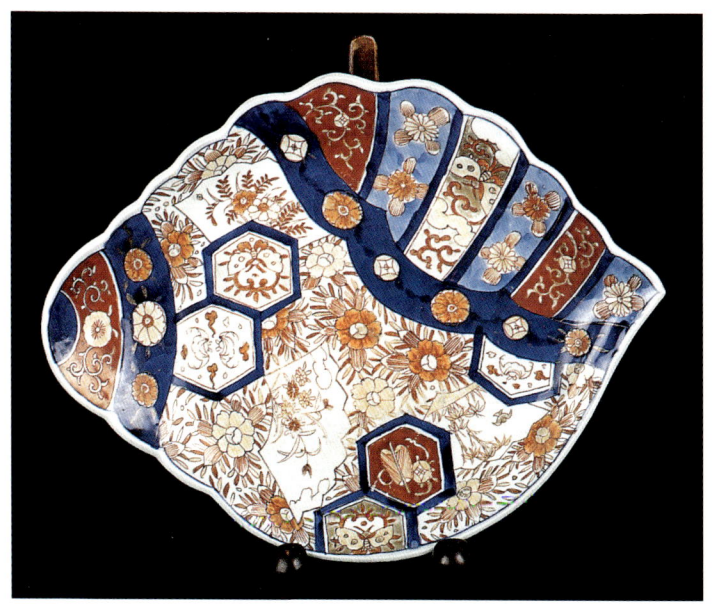

Imari shell-shaped dish with tapestry and floral decoration, 18" d. $725

Pair of leaf-shaped dishes decorated with two large fish and floral sprays, 12" l. $1,125

~ IMARI ~

Three fan-shaped Imari plates, 11" w. Set of six $2,575

Shell-shaped Imari dish with ho-ho bird, garden, and dragon decorations in reserves, 19.25" w. $1,775

Square Imari dish with central floral decoration, 13.5" w. $975

~ IMARI ~

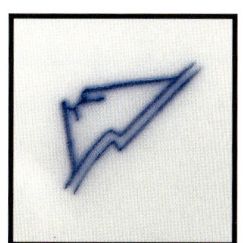

Top: One of a pair of square Imari platters with basket and floral arrangement in the center and floral band on the scalloped and segmented octagonal rim, c. 1860, 17" square. $8,855

Bottom: Fukagawa dish on three legs with scalloped rim and Kakiemon style polychrome rabbit and floral decoration, 5.75" d.
Collection of Tom & Linda Tompkins

~ IMARI ~

BOWLS

Large Imari bowl painted with scenes of people on the outside and with people and horses on the interior. 13.75" w. $1,950

Above & opposite: Large Imari bowl with tapestry patterns and decoration of cranes and flowers, c. 1840, 12.5" h. and 19" d. $10,465

~ IMARI ~

~ 45 ~

~ IMARI ~

Octagonal bowl with floral decoration, 11.75" d. $975

Fukagawa bowl with dancing butterfly design, c. 1880.
Courtesy Fukagawa Porcelain Manufacturing Co., Arita.

~ IMARI ~

Fukagawa tea bowl, plate, and pot with dancing butterfly design, c. 1880. *Courtesy Fukagawa Porcelain Manufacturing Co., Arita.*

Covered Imari bowl with lid which inverts to a serving dish, floral group and people in the decoration, 11" d. $800

~ IMARI ~

BOTTLES

Pair of double gourd Imari bottle vases with floral and bird decorations, 18.25" h. $4,830

~ IMARI ~

Pair of Imari double gourd bottle vases with pine, bamboo, and prune blossom decoration, birds and dragons, c. 1860, 19.5" h. $5,635

Pair of Imari bottle vases with garden railing and floral decoration, 12" h. $1,950

Pair of Imari bottle vases, 17" h., with bird and floral decoration. $4,025-4,830

~ IMARI ~

Large Koransha vase of unusually fine decoration with landscapes and vases with flowers in reserves and all-over floral and medallion decorations, c. 1880, 16.5" h. $3,060

~ 50 ~

~ IMARI ~

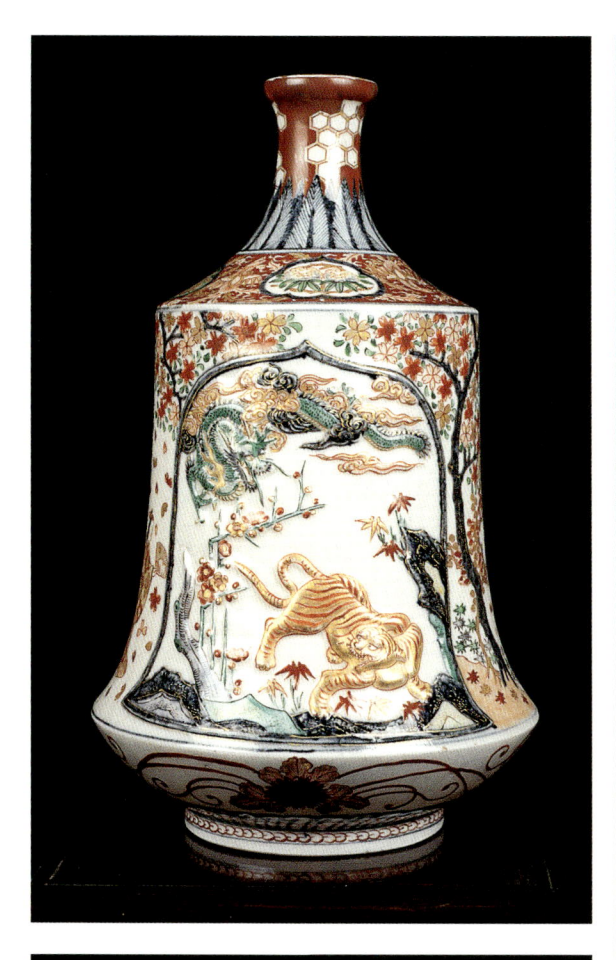

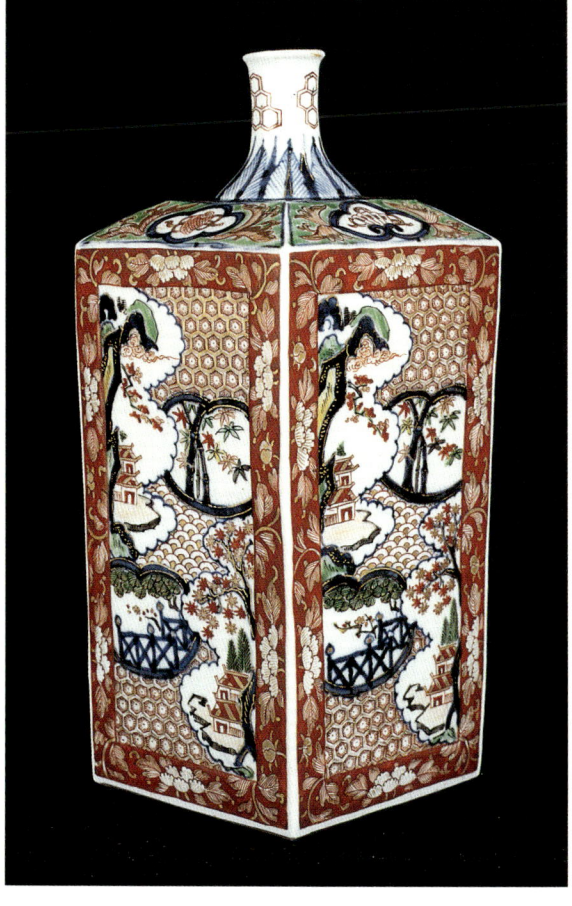

Top left: Imari bell-shaped bottle with raised and polychrome decoration of lion and dragon, floral borders, 19th century, 12.5" h. $3,220-4,025

Top right: Single Imari bottle and flat lid with orange and light blue painted decoration of landscape, people, and birds in reserves, 19.5" h. $1,450

Bottom left: Large Imari saki bottle of square shape with landscape and floral decoration, c. 1870, 9.75" h. $2,415

~ IMARI ~

VASES WITH FLORAL DECORATION

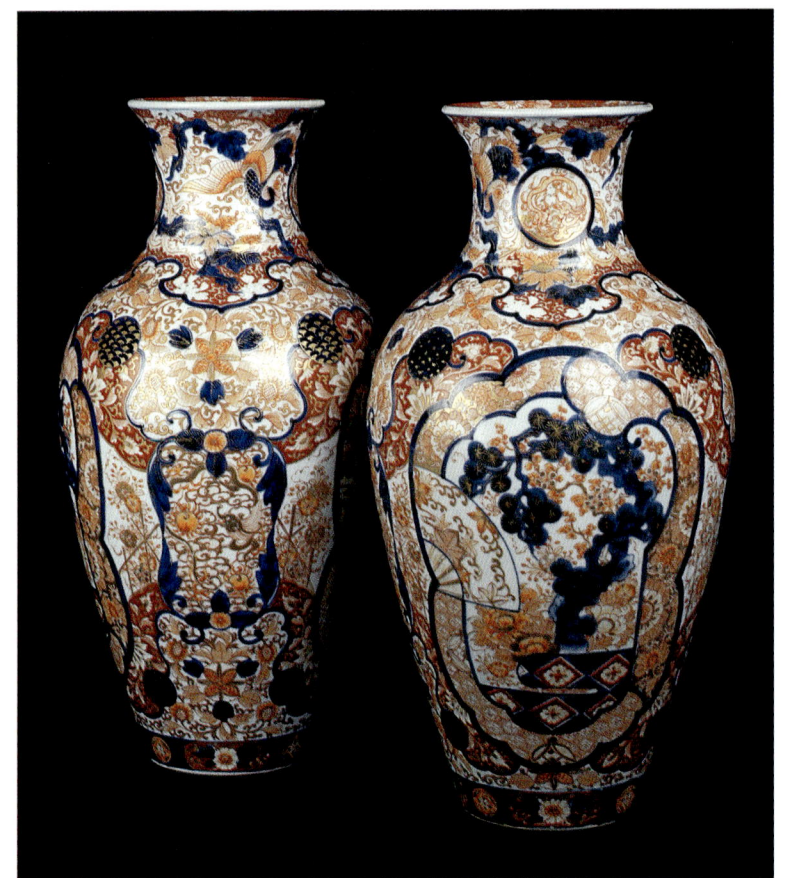

Top left: Pair of hexagonal vases with flaring rims, floral and three friends decoration, 14" h. $1,450

Top right: Pair of Imari, tall ribbed vases with flaring rims, pine and floral decoration, c. 1860, 20" h. $5,635

Bottom left: Pair of Imari vases with pine tree and fan decoration, 15.5" h. $2,900

~ IMARI ~

Pair of Imari vases with flaring rims and painted three friends and chrysanthemums decoration, 16" h. $2,175

Pair of Imari vases with ribbed sides and floral decoration, 10.75" h. $1,300

Pair of ribbed Imari vases with floral and bird decoration, 12" h. $1,950

Pair of Imari vases with floral and bird decoration, 12" h. $975

~ IMARI ~

Top left: Imari vase with floral decoration mounted as a table lamp, 11.5" h. $485

Top right: Pair of Imari vases with floral decoration and iron red background, 10.25" h. $1,130

Bottom: Pair of vases with ribbed sides and floral decoration, red orb and cross mark, 15.5" h. $2,560

~ IMARI ~

Top: Square Imari vase with floral and bird decoration and a relief band, 14" h. $2,575

Bottom left: Pair of scalloped Imari vases, 14.25" h. $2,250

Bottom right: Pair of Imari vases with pastel floral and bird decoration, 15" h. $245

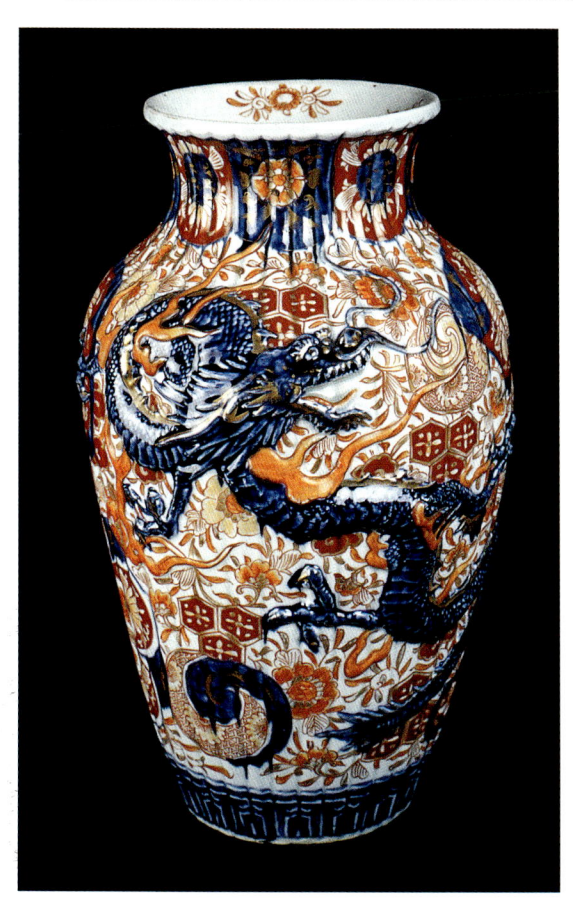

~ 55 ~

~ IMARI ~

Fukagawa Imari vase with floral decoration
and thick gold painted rim, 9.75" h. $1,450

Tall Koransha oval vase with a floral arrangement in
a vase and bird decoration, c. 1880, 18.5" h. $8,050

~ IMARI ~

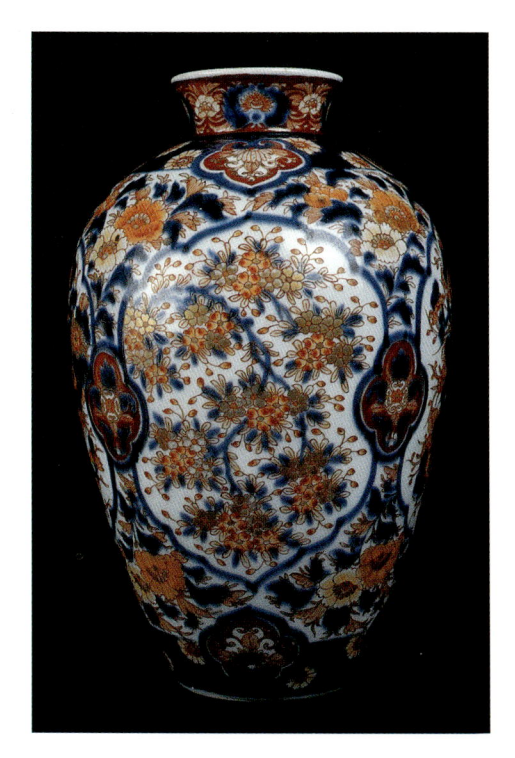

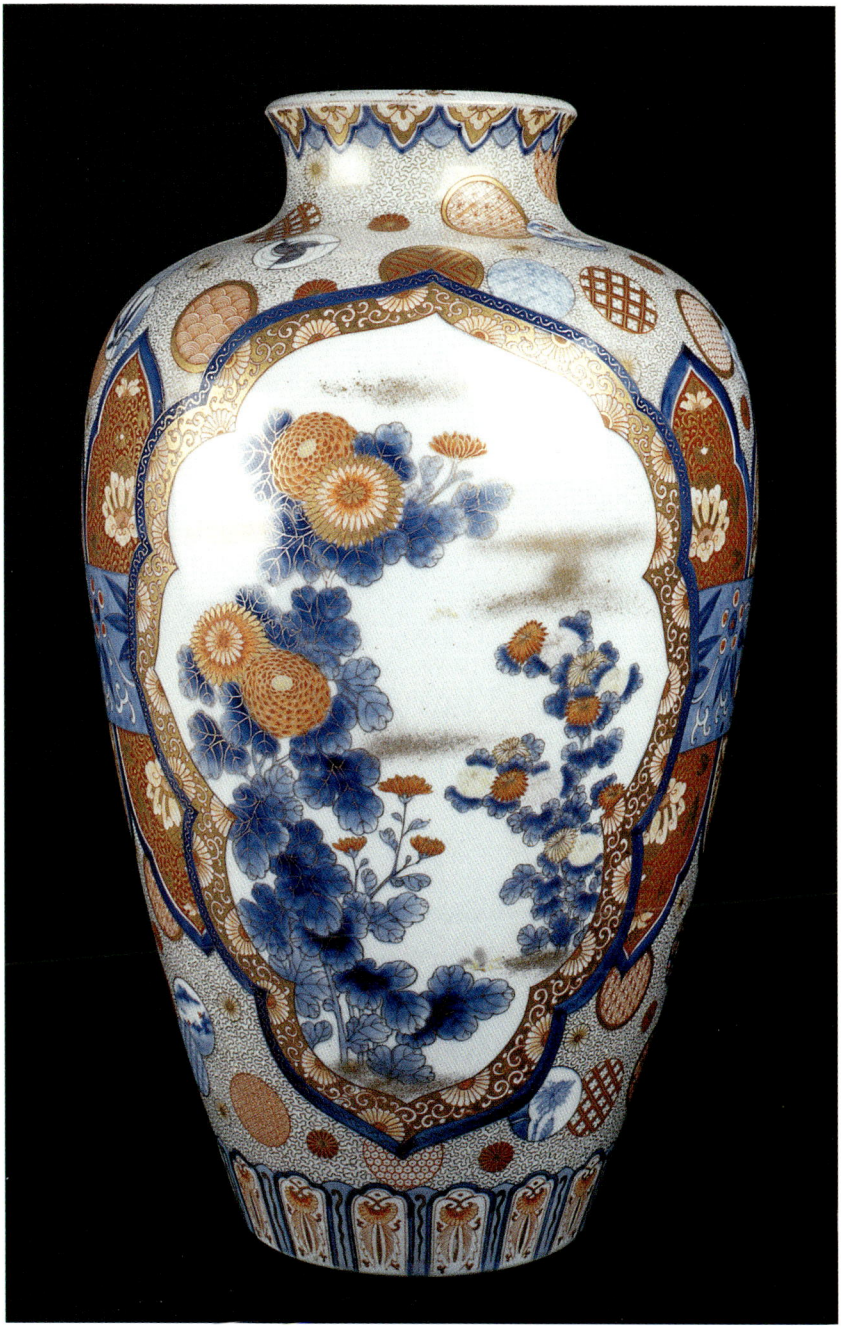

Top left: Single Fukagawa Imari vase decorated with floral painting, four character red mark, 10.5" h. $485

Top right: Fukagawa vase with reserves of floral and bamboo grove decoration, 17.75" h. $1,775

Bottom left: Single Koransha floral and ho-ho bird decorated vase, c. 1880, 12" h. $965

~ IMARI ~

Small vase with blue shaded glaze and white relief chicken decoration, 3.75" h. *Collection of Tom & Linda Tompkins*

Miniature porcelain vase in green with shaded floral decoration by studio artist Shufu, 3.75" h. Miniature porcelain vase in green with bamboo decoration by studio artist Enji Nishiura, 3.5" h. *Collection of Tom & Linda Tompkins*

Nabeshima jar/vase with red floral overglaze and blue underglaze tree decoration, base marked in blue, c. 1860-70, 6.25" h. *Collection of Tom & Linda Tompkins*

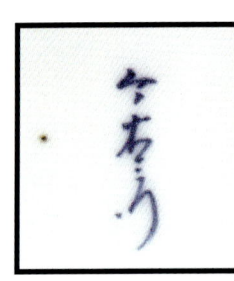

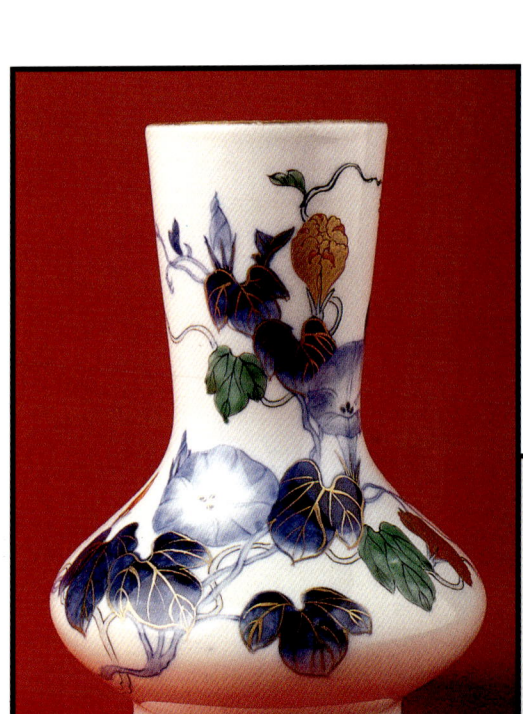

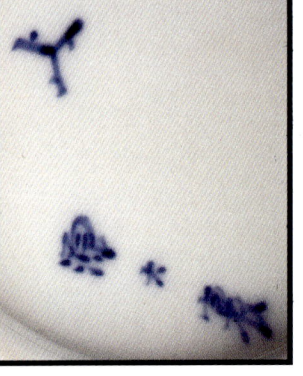

Imari vase decorated with polychrome overglaze and blue underglaze in morning glories floral design, marked by Tominiga Genroku, 7.5" h. *Collection of Tom & Linda Tompkins*

~ 58 ~

~ IMARI ~

VASES WITH PEOPLE DECORATION

Pair of Imari vases decorated with panels depicting a standing man with a walking stick and a young boy among floral details, 12" h. $975

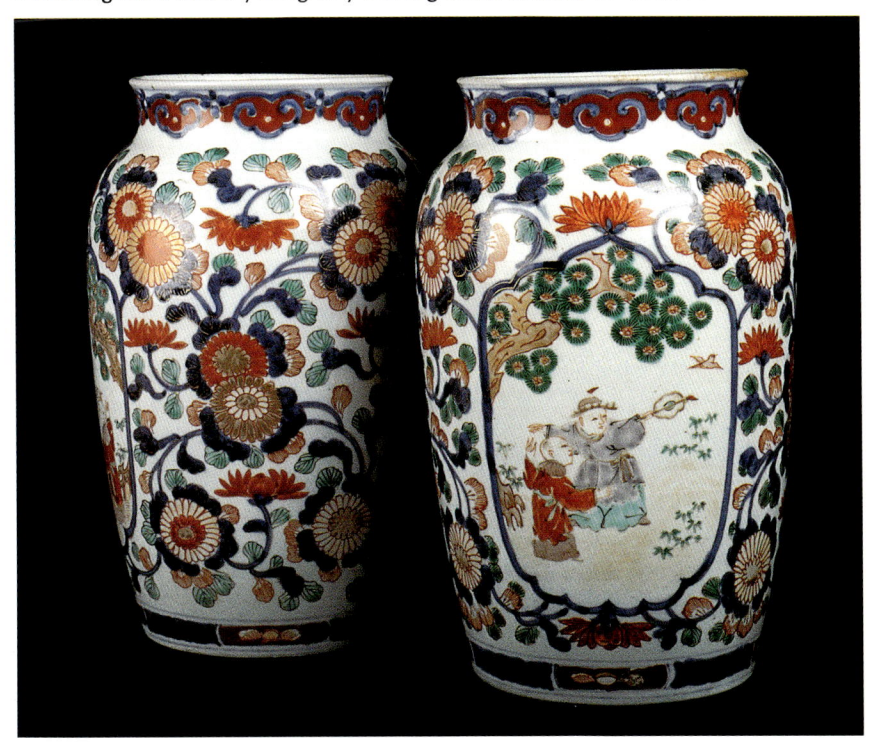

Pair of Imari vases decorated with scenes of two boys hunting birds, 10" h. $970

~ IMARI ~

Pair of Imari vases with all-over floral decoration and reserves painted with cranes on one side and group of women in a garden on the other side, 17.75" h. $1,610

Pair of vases with decoration of two women and a boat, 18" h. $2,095

Pair of Koransha Imari vases painted with two scenes of an old man in a garden, c. 1880, 11" h., red mark. $1,775

~ IMARI ~

Above: Pair of Fukagawa vases showing children at play against red background, c. 1880. *Courtesy of Fukagawa Porcelain Manufacturing Co., Arita.*

Right: Fukagawa Imari porcelain vase with fluted and flaring rim, and two landscape panels with men or women, 26" h., red 6-character mark.

~ IMARI ~

VASES WITH BIRDS DECORATION

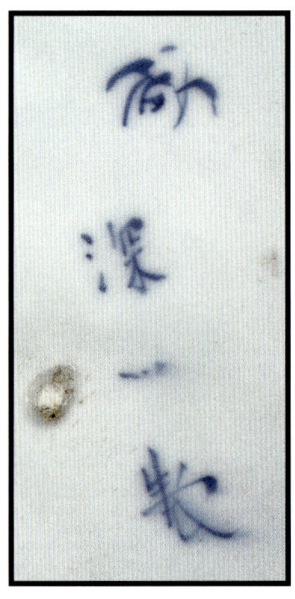

Tall vase of oval form with cranes and birds in a floral setting, c. 1880, 18.25" h. $3,220

Fukagawa urn with four panels decorated with river landscape, ho-ho bird, bamboo grove, and floral painting, 10" h. $1,125

~ IMARI ~

VASES WITH DRAGONS DECORATION

Top: Pair of Imari vases of urn shape with side handles and scalloped rim, dragon and butterfly design, c. 1900, probably made by Fukagawa but not marked, 18.5" h. $4,830

Bottom left: Fukagawa Imari porcelain jug with one handle and unusual painted dragon decoration, c. 1880, 10.5" h. $245

Bottom right: Fukagawa fan-shaped vase with green dragon design and large blue mark, c. 1900-1920, 8.15" h. *Collection of Tom & Linda Tompkins*

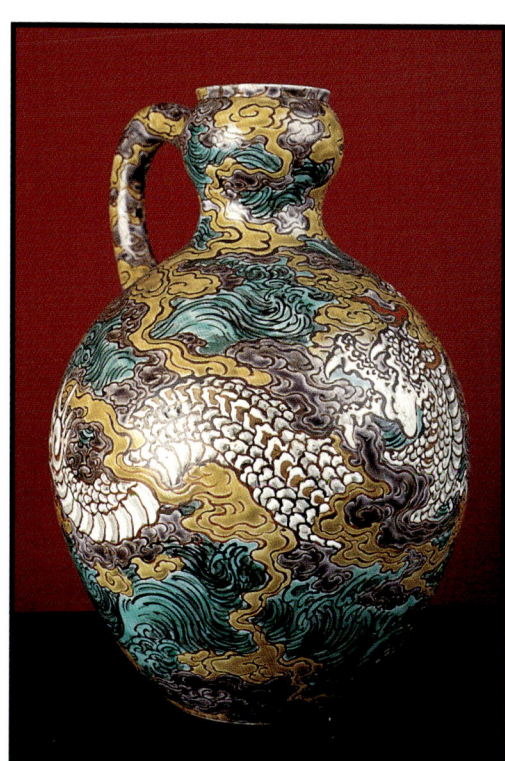

~ 63 ~

~ IMARI ~

VASES WITH FISH DECORATION

Pair of vases with fish decoration, Koransha blue mark, c. 1880, 12.5" h. $2,898

~ IMARI ~

Left: Koransha vase with brown matte decoration and fish and floral decoration, c. 1880, 22.25" h. $4,025

Below: Fukagawa Imari porcelain vase with reserves of fish and bamboo grove, blue mark, 15" h. $1,450

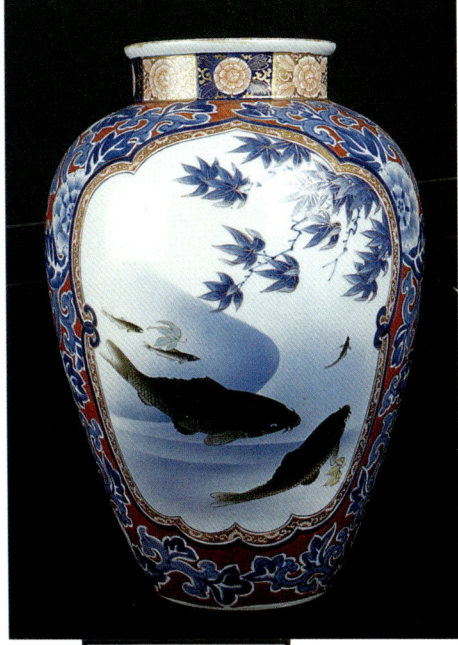

~ IMARI ~

JARS AND GARNITURE

Top: Pair of Imari covered jars with two panels of vase and floral arrangement decoration and two panels of landscapes with horses, people, and buildings, 22.5" h.

Bottom: Pair of Imari covered urns with floral decoration, 12.5" h. $1,450

~ IMARI ~

Top left: Pair of old Imari covered urns with red floral and lion decoration lightly painted, blue background in the shoulder and domed lid, with white lion finials, 15.5" h. $3,220

Top right: Pair of small Imari ribbed covered urns with decorated foo dog finials, 13" h. $975

Bottom: Pair of Imari covered urns with ribbed sides and all-over architectural decoration, 18" h. $4,025

~ IMARI ~

Top left: Pair of Imari covered urns with sixteen ribbed sides and floral and architectural decoration, 16" h. $2,900

Center right: Two similar covered urns with ribbed sides, tapestry and floral decoration, 12.5 and 11.5" h. For two $1,290

Bottom: Pair of Imari covered jars with bird and floral decoration, 16.5" h.

~ 68 ~

~ IMARI ~

Top: Large Imari vase with floral spray in the reserves and landscape with flowers in the shoulder, c. 1680-1700, 19.5" h. $8,050

Bottom: Porcelain covered bowl with underglaze blue, gold, and polychrome floral decoration and a foo-dog finial, 11" h. *Collection of Tom & Linda Tompkins*

~ IMARI ~

Pair of covered jars with gray dragons decoration, Koransha red mark, c. 1880, 12.5" h. $3,220-4,025

Fukagawa temple jar of European eighteenth-century shape decorated with "Blue China" design which was shown at the 1900 Paris World Exposition. *Courtesy of Fukagawa Porcelain Manufacturing Company, Arita.*

~ 70 ~

– IMARI –

SPECIALTY SHAPES

Two Imari pagoda lanterns, 18" h. $4,190

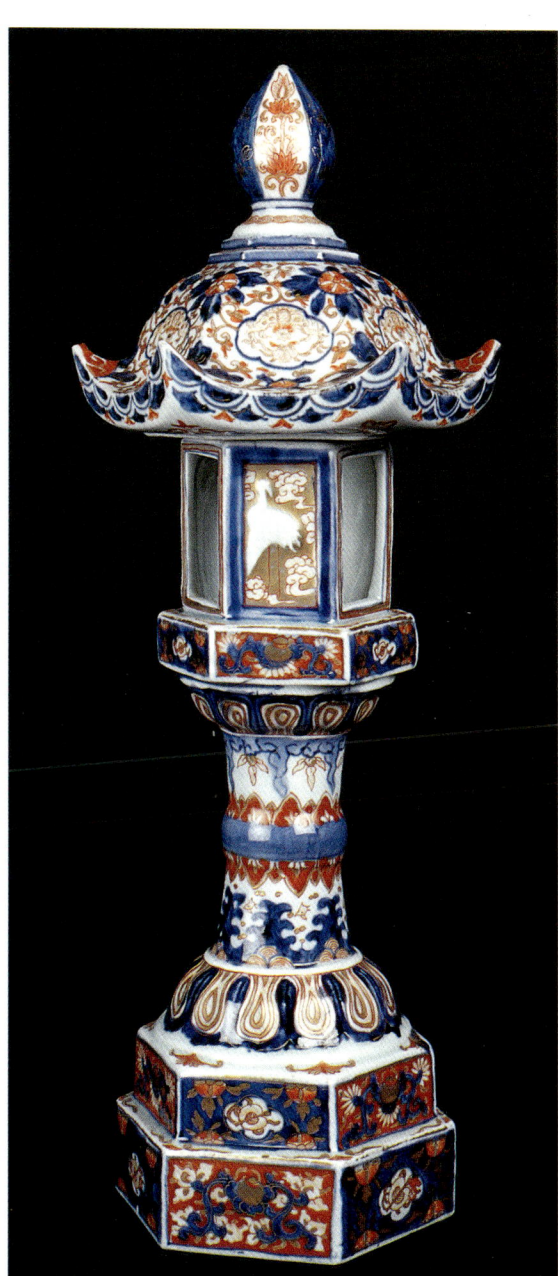

Single Imari lantern, 17.5" h. $1,950

~ IMARI ~

Top left: Imari jug with hole for a metal tap and a loop to attach the lid, floral gold sprays in white reserves with blue borders, 13" h. $4,025

Center right: Koransha tea pot with bamboo-wrapped bail handle, globular body decorated with blue medallion and overglaze enamels, c. 1880, 4.5" h. *Collection of Tom & Linda Tompkins*

Bottom: Fukagawa covered rectangular box with ribbon and blue floral decoration, c. 1880. *Courtesy of Fukagawa Porcelain Manufacturing Company, Arita.*

HIRADO PORCELAIN

Hirado Island was an early Portuguese settlement in the mid-seventeenth century and became a place where Christianity was embraced by many Japanese. Here the Dutch East India Company established a trading center in the mid-seventeenth century and fine Hirado porcelain, from a local factory, was included among the exports to the West before 1688. Later, exports of Hirado ware were relatively rare, until the last half of the nineteenth century, as most of the production was consumed in the Japanese domestic trade.

Hirado porcelain is characterized by thin and highly refined white clay that would be fired to high temperatures. The clay was dense enough to hold fine details and supported finely painted underglaze blue decoration. Figurines as well as dish forms were made for gifts to the Japanese leaders and as trade items, especially in the last quarter of the nineteenth century.

FIGURES

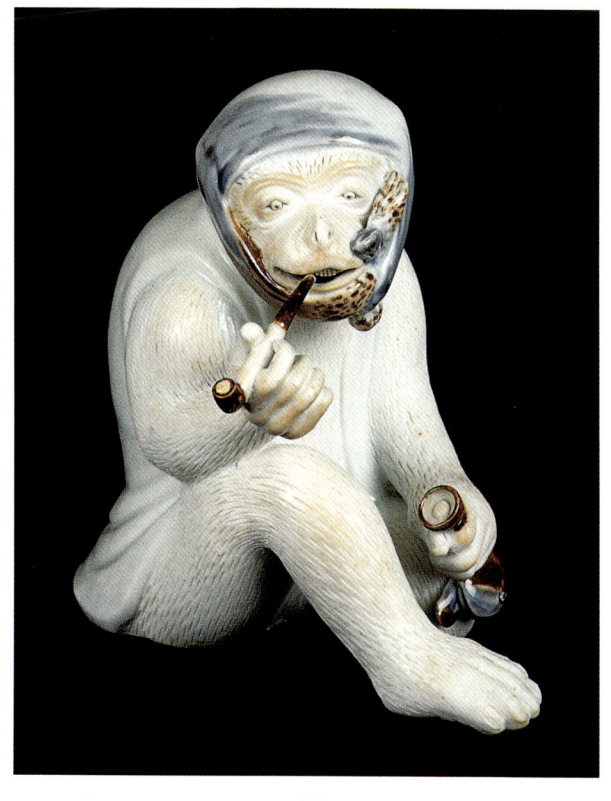

Hirado monkey figure with blood-stained bandanna, holding a pouch, and smoking a pipe, 6.5" h. $1610

~ HIRADO ~

Hirado horse figure, 6.5" h. $3220

Two pair of Hirado figurines or figural water droppers as seated dogs. *Collection of Tom & Linda Tompkins*

Three Hirado miniature figurines: crouching lion, man with a beast, dragon. *Collection of Tom & Linda Tompkins*

~ HIRADO ~

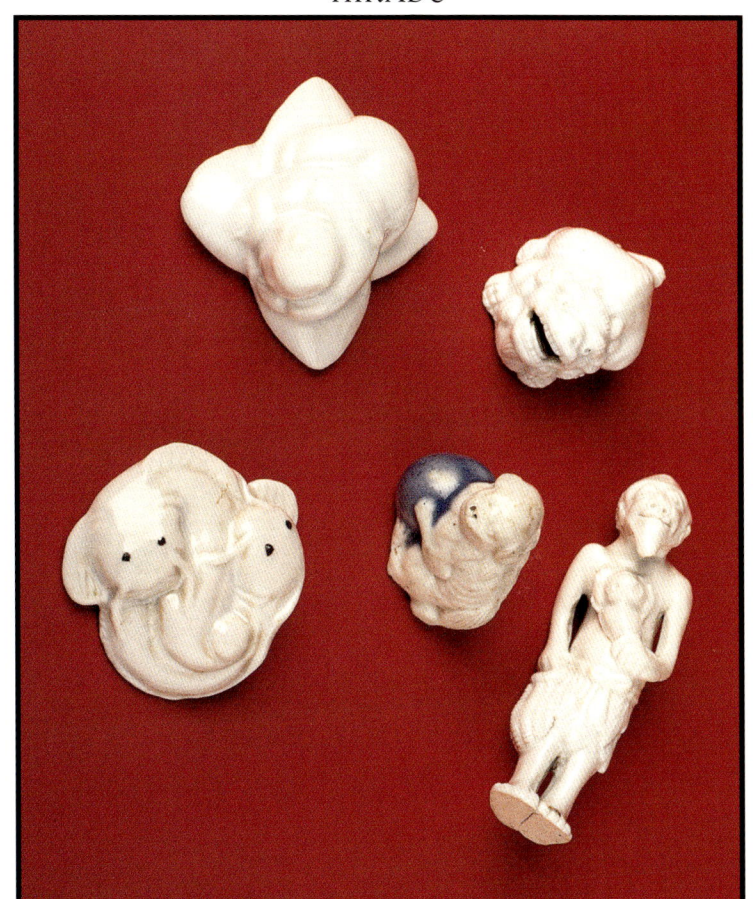

Top: Group of Hirado netsuke in figural shapes: crouching boy, lion with ball in its mouth, two carp intertwined, dog with blue ball, standing man holding a fish. *Collection of Tom & Linda Tompkins*

Center: Four small porcelain figurines: Hirado reclining young boy, Hirado fish with one boy riding on its back and another boy hiding in its mouth, polychrome Hotei figure, Celadon Hotei figure. *Collection of Tom & Linda Tompkins*

Bottom: Solid clay figurine of a goat with blue details, late Hirado period. *Collection of Tom & Linda Tompkins*

~ HIRADO ~

Hirado foo dog figure, 5.5" h. $2,575

Pair of Hirado figures of seated dogs with blue details, female with open mouth, 4.5" h. *Collection of Tom & Linda Tompkins*

Hirado porcelain figurine of Hotei with walking stick and fabric sack, 9" h. *Collection of Tom & Linda Tompkins*

~ HIRADO ~

Pair of Hirado figurines of a man and a woman, 6.25" h.

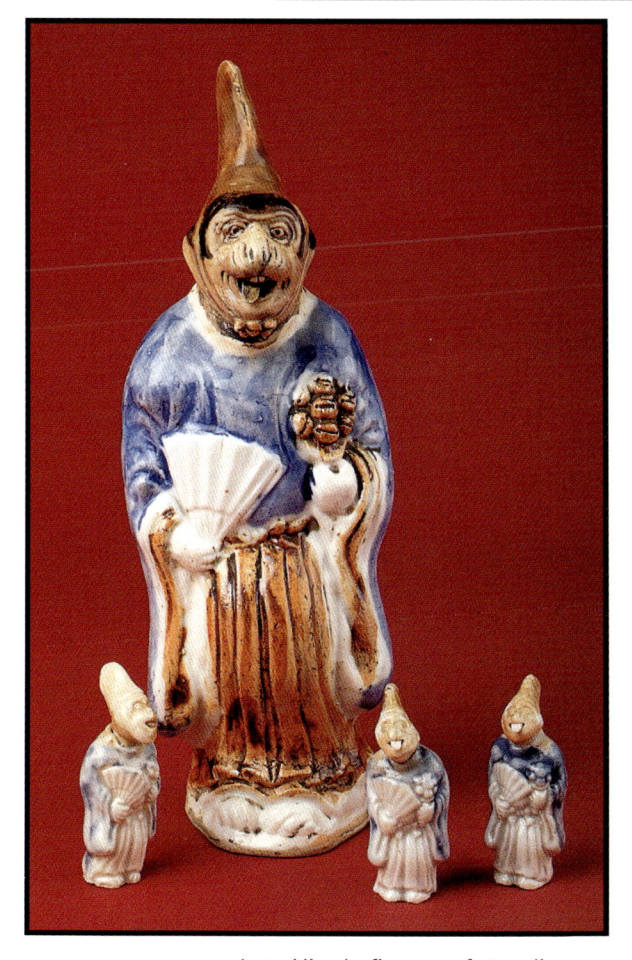

Late Hirado figures of standing men with nodding heads and protruding flat tongues, c. 1920, ranging in height from 2.25" h. to 5.75" h.
Left: *Collection of Tom & Linda Tompkins*. Right: *Collection of W. Parker*

~ HIRADO ~

PLATES, ROUND

Hirado plate with blue decoration of fantastic animal and bats in the rim, 9.25" d. *Collection of Tom & Linda Tompkins*

Hirado plate with raised and painted floral decoration, 8.25" d. *Collection of Tom & Linda Tompkins*

~ HIRADO ~

Hirado dish, 7" d., and three bowls, 5" and 5.75" d., each with floral decoration but not matching. *Collection of Tom & Linda Tompkins*

Hirado or unmarked Fukagawa dish with raised and blue and green painted landscape decoration, 7.5" d. *Collection of Tom & Linda Tompkins*

Above: Miniature Hirado dishes: plate with three boys playing in the blue decoration, 4" d.; two open bowls with decoration of five boys, 2.5" d.; covered bowl with decoration in round medallions, 1.5" d. *Collection of Tom & Linda Tompkins*

~ HIRADO ~

PLATES, SHAPED

Right: Hirado square dish on raised foot with building in landscape decoration, 5.5" square. *Collection of Tom & Linda Tompkins*

Footed Hirado dish with four lobes and fine blue waves and floral decoration, 6.25" l. *Collection of Tom & Linda Tompkins*

Boat-shaped, Hirado dish with interior "three friends" decoration (bamboo, pine and plum trees), and exterior painted with figures in a landscape, c. 1840-70, 7" l. x 2.4" h. *Collection of Tom & Linda Tompkins*

~ HIRADO ~

BOWLS

Hirado cup with short footed base and straight flaring sides decorated with two bands of relief geometric patterns and blue bird and floral design, 3.85" h. *Collection of Tom & Linda Tompkins*

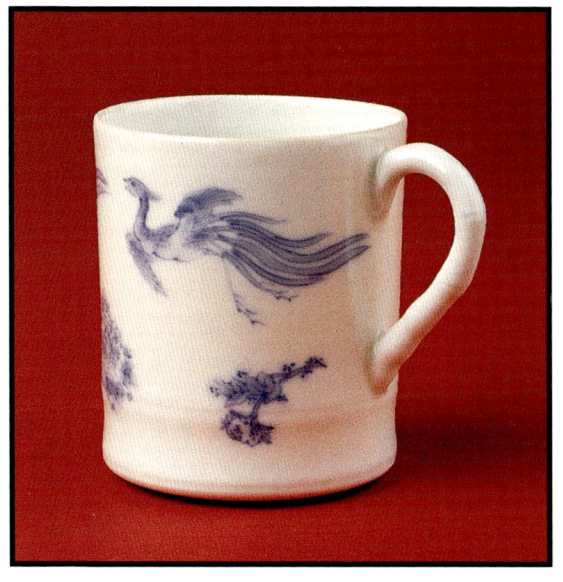

Straight sided Hirado mug with curved handle and three ho-ho birds with floral sprays in the blue decoration, 2.5" h. *Collection of Tom & Linda Tompkins*

BOTTLES

Hirado gourd-shaped bottle with blue "three friends" decoration (bamboo, pine and plum trees), 8.5" h. *Collection of Tom & Linda Tompkins*

Hirado saki bottle with spout and tall neck over a wide round body decorated with pine fronds, 5" h. *Collection of Tom & Linda Tompkins*

~ 81 ~

~ HIRADO ~

VASES

Hirado hanging vase of square shape with landscape decoration, 5.75" h. *Collection of Tom & Linda Tompkins*

Above & opposite: Hirado vase and figure group of seven scholars and a child around a bamboo grove with blue leaves, 11.5" h. $4,025-4,830

~ HIRADO ~

~ 83 ~

~ HIRADO ~

JARS

Hirado jar for fresh water used in the tea ceremony (*mizusashi*) of square shape and decorated with bamboo stems and leaves, c. 1800, 7" h. *Collection of Tom & Linda Tompkins*

Hirado covered jar with flying cranes decoration in underglaze blue, 11" h. $3,550

Above & right: Hirado jar for fresh water used in the tea ceremony (*mizusashi*) of ovoid shape and decorated with landscape scene of buildings and mountains, c. 1870, impressed mark on base, 7.5" h. *Collection of Tom & Linda Tompkins*

~ 84 ~

HIRADO

Above: Lid of a Hirado water pot with figural lion finial and blue moon and plover decoration, 4.25" d. *Collection of Tom & Linda Tompkins*

Right: Large Hirado covered bowl with painted blue dragon decoration and a relief dragon coiled around the lid and bowl, 10" h. *Collection of Tom & Linda Tompkins*

Four Hirado incense burners, each with reticulated lids. *Back:* The largest of bird shape on raised base with turtle finial, 5.25" h. *Left:* The solid base on three peg feet with decoration of tree and *shishi* mask handles, c. 1830-60, 3.7" h. *Center:* The reticulated base on three peg feet with salamander handles, c. 1850-80, 3" h. *Right:* The solid base on three peg feet with painted decoration of large birds and *shishi* mask handles, c. 1830-60, 4.25" h. *Collection of Tom & Linda Tompkins*

~ HIRADO ~

SPECIALTY SHAPES

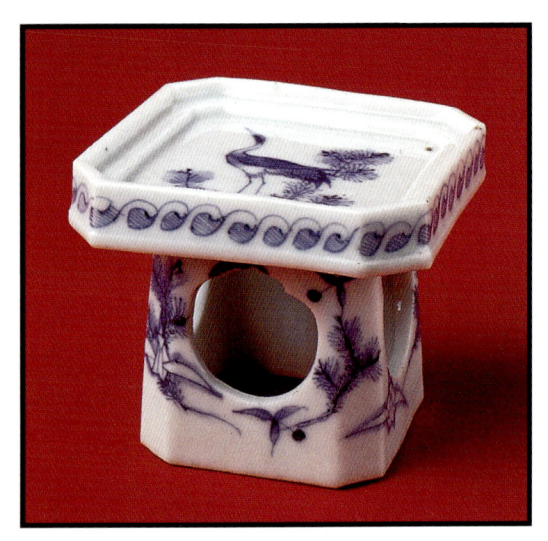

Hirado stand with octagonal base pierced on four sides supporting a solid octagonal top with blue bird decoration, 2.75" h. *Collection of Tom & Linda Tompkins*

Hirado stand for an important object with figural base including a man riding a sea turtle, oval flat surface above with a gallery on two sides, 5.25" h. *Collection of Tom & Linda Tompkins*

Hirado 4-lobed teapot on four peg feet with squared handle and round lid, decorated with blue underglaze children playing with butterflies, c. 1840-70, 5" h. *Collection of Tom & Linda Tompkins*

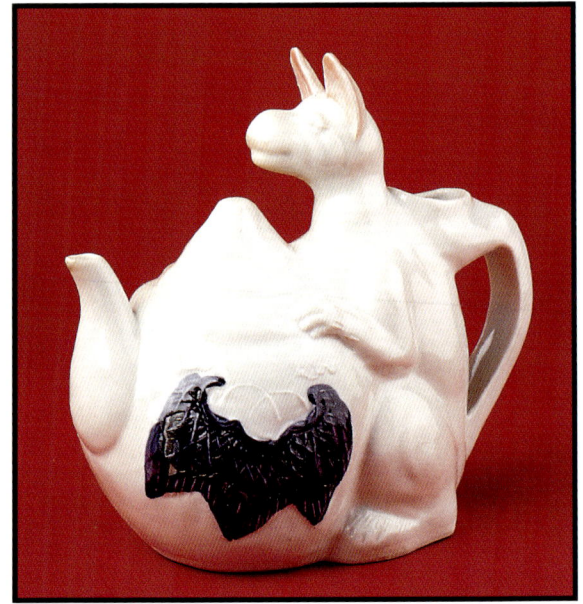

Hirado teapot molded with an imaginary animal figure with pink ears and pot with blue bat decoration on the sides, 6.85" h. *Collection of Tom & Linda Tompkins*

~ HIRADO ~

Hirado water dropper in the shape of a turtle with a handle, 4.25" h. Hirado bonbon dish with handle and two clusters of finely detailed relief chrysanthemums attached, 5" l. *Collection of Tom & Linda Tompkins*

Hirado tea pot designed as the god of Propriety, Ibisu, with a fish, c. 1920, 4.25" h. *Meyers-Voll Collection*

Hirado tea pot in the form of a fish with a man riding on its back, 5.5" h. *Meyers-Voll Collection*

Kutani Porcelain

Many styles of Kutani porcelain decoration were centered in the rice-growing Kaga province, and may originally have developed to sustain trade in rice for undecorated ceramics from areas such as Arita. Diverse styles and qualities of decoration are associated with Kutani, the most frequent being elaborate red designs. Kutani decoration is not so frequently found on the market today as Imari or Satsuma, and the variable quality of the decoration makes it generally less valuable than the other styles. Individual pieces must be considered on their own merits, for there are many Kutani porcelains of exceptional quality, in both shapes and decorations.

FIGURES

Pair of Kutani figures of a girl and a boy holding large bells on their shoulders, c. 1800, 11.25" h.

~ KUTANI ~

Pair of Kutani standing figures with large jars which are decorated with green landscapes, 10.25" h. $1,320

Kutani figure of a seated woman, 6.75" h. *Collection of W. Parker*

Kutani covered dish depicting Hotei and his very large cloth bag, 5.25" l. $565

~ KUTANI ~

Top left: Kutani figure group of two men, 10.25" h. $1,950

Top right: Kutani standing figure of a woman with a fan, 12" h. $650

Bottom: Kutani figure of monkey and baby, 11.25" l. $5,635

~ 91 ~

~ KUTANI ~

PLATES, ROUND

Three round Kutani plates with scenes of Samurai in landscapes signed by Nakamura, Yokahama, late 19th century, 7" d. *Courtesy of Marvin Baer*

Kutani relief plaque showing a woman in a garden setting, 12.5" d. c, 1900. *Courtesy of Marvin Baer*

Kutani dish with red painted decoration of a man in a grass hut and rice field, 9.75" d. *Collection of Tom & Linda Tompkins*

~ 92 ~

~ KUTANI ~

PLATES, SHAPED

Kutani covered squid-shaped dish, 10" l. $800

Kutani plate shaped as a bird's head painted in red and gold, back marked, 10" l. *Collection of W. Parker*

Kutani diamond-shaped dish painted with red shrimp in the base and rim design of ribbons and dots, 7.3" l. *Drick-Messing Collection*

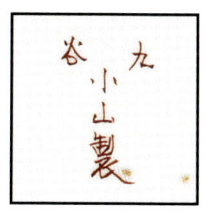

~ 93 ~

~ KUTANI ~

BOTTLES

Pair of Kutani covered bottle vases with seated Hotei figural finials, 19.5" h. $2,420

~ KUTANI ~

Kutani saki bottles with painted brown landscape decoration, bases with rims cut out before the final glaze was applied, 6" h. *Drick-Messing Collection*

Kutani bottle with two frogs on the shoulder and textured background with pointed leaf and insect applied relief decoration, 4" h. *Collection of W. Parker*

~ 95 ~

~ KUTANI ~

VASES

Top: Pair of bulbous Kutani vases with painted bird decoration, 10.5" h. $1,125

Bottom: Pair of Kutani straight-sided vases with black bands at the tops and bottoms and standing men in the center, 13" h. $650

~ KUTANI ~

Top: Pair of Kutani vases decorated with scholars and tiger polychrome decoration, 14" h. $1,530

Bottom left: Kutani vase with orange background and many floral-decorated reserves, 12" h. $325

Bottom right: Pair of Kutani bottle-shaped vases painted with floral decoration, 12" h. *Courtesy of Marvin Baer*

~ KUTANI ~

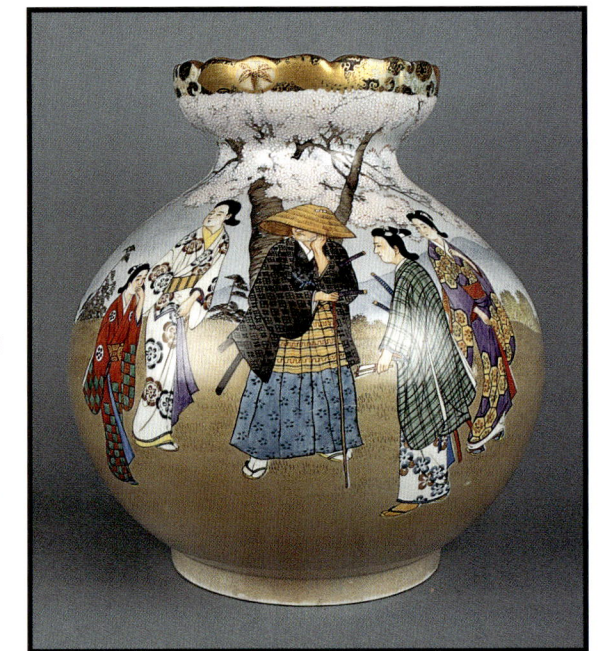

Top: Kutani vase of bulbous shape decorated with painted decoration of five women in a landscape with cherry trees, 12.25" h. *Courtesy of Marvin Baer*

Bottom left: Pair of Kutani vases decorated with a green sea and water creatures and dragon, 15.75" h. $1,950

Bottom right: Kutani vase decorated with pastel bird and floral design interrupted with diagonal insets of different floral design, 18.5" h. $1,450

~ KUTANI ~

Top: Pair of Kutani vases with fan-shaped reserves containing flowers and scenes with people, 14.5" h. $1,050

Bottom left: Pair of Kutani vases with children and adults in landscapes, 15.75" h. $1,530

Bottom right: Pair of Kutani vases with bird and floral decoration, 14.5" h.

~ KUTANI ~

Top: Pair of Kutani vases with bird and floral pastel decoration on white ground, 13" h. $1,375

Bottom left: Kutani vase with painted reserves and relief fan decoration, c. 1900, 11" h. *Courtesy of Marvin Baer* $850-950

Bottom right: Pair of Kutani vases on three feet of crouching bears, each vase with three oval panels of important people, 10" h. $1,530

~ KUTANI ~

Above: Kutani diamond-shaped, tall flaring vase with finely painted gold, red, and black decoration.

Left: Kutani vase of exceptional quality with separate stand, c. 1870, 17.25" h. $3,220-4,025

~ KUTANI ~

Pair of tall Kutani vases with people depicted in the reserves, c. 1860-70, 17" h. $8,050

~ KUTANI ~

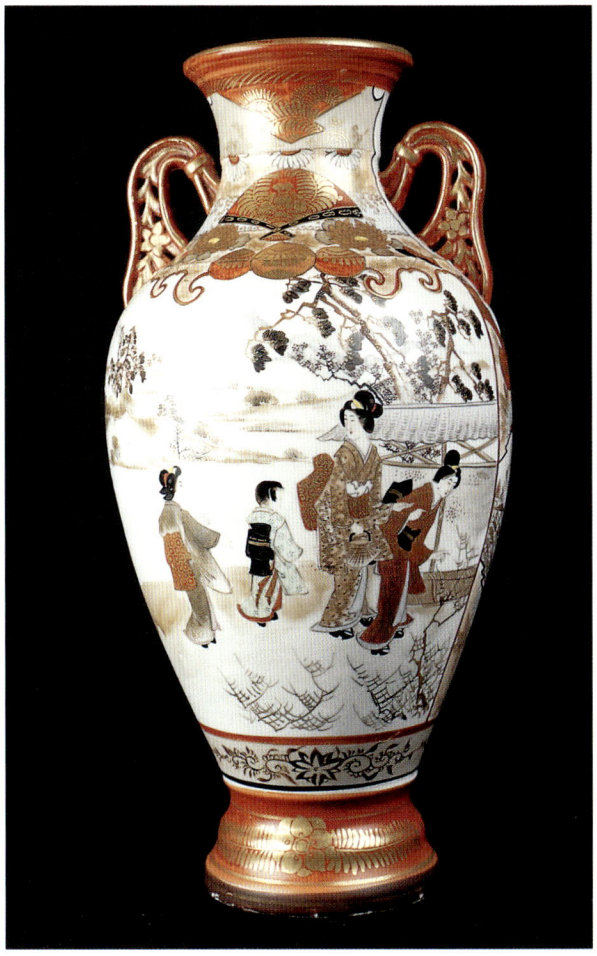

Top left: Pair of Kutani vases with mask and ring handles and decoration of peacocks and women decoration, 13.25" h. $2,575

Top right: Kutani vase with pierced handles and decoration of women and children in landscapes, 14.5" h. $1,200

Bottom: Pair of Kutani vases with fish handles and decorated with red spotted lions and gray dragons, 13.25" h. $1,450

~ KUTANI ~

Top: Pair of Kutani vases with portraits of women among floral vines and birds, 15.5" h. $1,200

Bottom left: Pair of Kutani vases with decoration of people among cherry blossoms, 14.5" h. $885

Bottom right: Kutani vase with footed base, two rectangular handles at the neck, painted in gold and polychrome to show a standing man, a crawling woman, and a seated man, 15.5" h. *Courtesy of Marvin Baer* $1350-1500

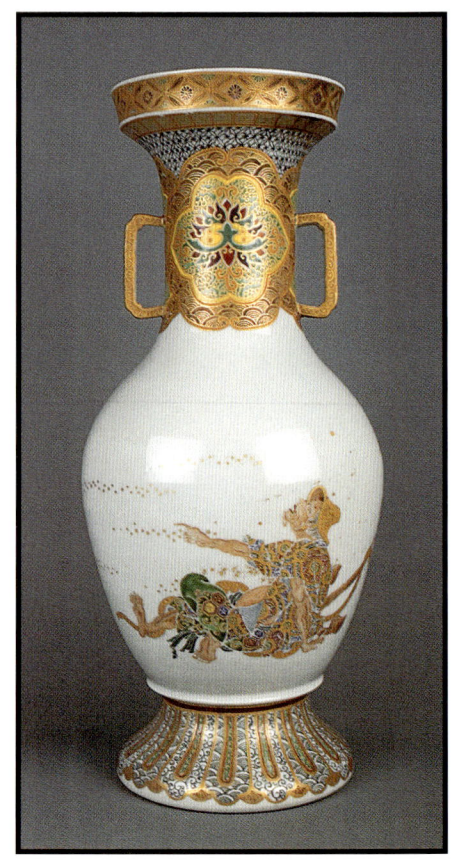

~ 104 ~

~ KUTANI ~

Pair of Kutani vases of ovoid shape with painted decoration of fish, handles shaped as elephant heads with rings. *Courtesy of Marvin Baer.*

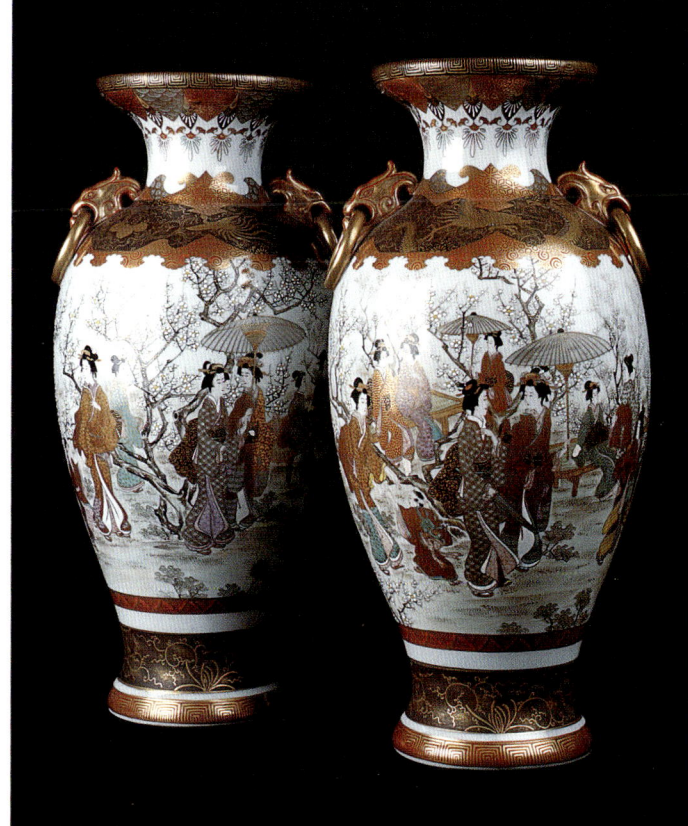

Pair of Kutani vases with gold ring handles and a procession of people, 13.5" h. $2,415

Pair of large Kutani vases with fluted rims and floral decoration, 24.5" h. $2,420

~ KUTANI ~

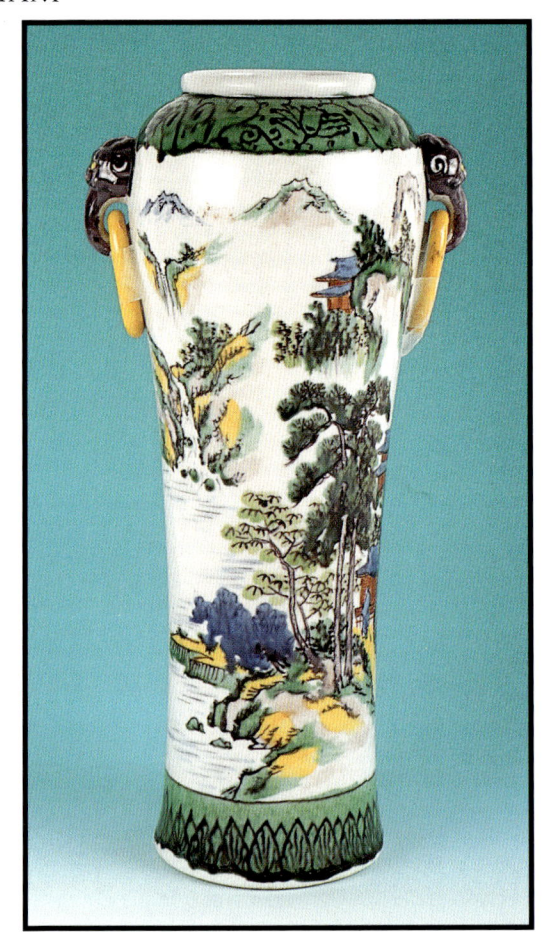

Top left: Single Kutani vase with mask and ring handles and knotted tassels, 14.5" h. $565

Top right: Kutani tall and bulbous vase with painted landscape decoration and elephant head handles with gold rings, 11.25" h. *Courtesy of Marvin Baer*

JARS

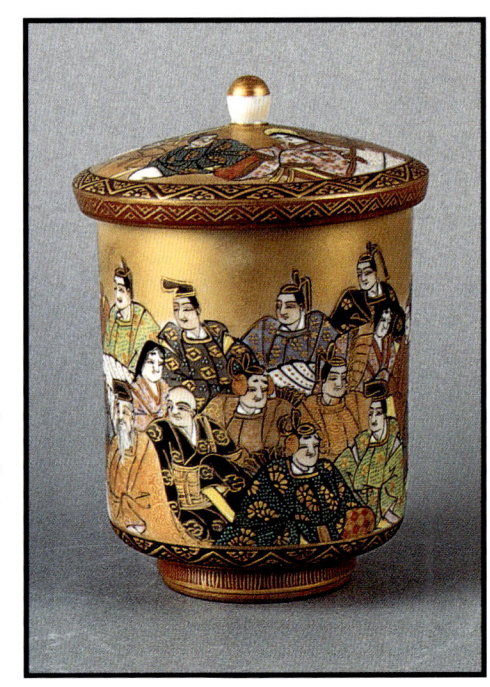

Small Kutani covered jar decorated with the images of 36 poets on the outside and inscriptions on the inside, 4" h. x 3" d. *Drick-Messing Collection*

SATSUMA EARTHENWARE

Satsuma earthenware is recognized today as low-fired ceramic ware with crackled glaze and detailed polychrome decoration. Two styles are generally identified: Kagoshima-style and Kyoto-style Satsuma.

Kagoshima-style wares were made in the Satsuma province in the southern part of Kyushu under the patronage of the Prince of Satsuma and date not before the early nineteenth century.

Kyoto-style Satsuma was made in a new "antique style" from about 1870 until about 1915. It utilized a variety of clays and/or bisque fired blanks transported to Kyoto by individual potters and was decorated by specialized artists. Kyoto-Satsuma wares were exported to the West in large numbers roughly between 1875 and 1920.

Production artists of Kyoto-style Satsuma wares had workshops in leading trade centers, such as Kyoto, Yokohama, and Osaka, to keep up with the export demand. Some of the decorators can be identified by their markings on the pieces. While most Kyoto-style Satsuma bears hand-painted floral decoration, Yabu Meizan, a particularly prolific decorator, used copper plate prints of detailed designs that were then finely painted on the crackled glaze of the soft earthenware's surface. (See Yabu Meizan section to follow.)

~ SATSUMA ~

FIGURES OF WOMEN

Above: Satsuma figure of a woman offering her breast to a young boy, 11.5" h. *Collection of Tom & Linda Tompkins*

Right: Satsuma figure of a standing woman holding an animal, 9.25" h. $2,750

~ SATSUMA ~

Satsuma figure of a standing woman with floral coat, 7.25" h.

Satsuma figure of a standing woman holding flowers, 12" h. $3,220-4,025

~ SATSUMA ~

Above: Kagoshima Satsuma figure of two standing women, 11.5" h. $4,025-4,800

Left: Mark of blue cross and two lines of gold characters.

薩摩焼
集穂

Satsuma figure of a standing woman holding a fan, 18.5" h. $5,635-6,440

~ SATSUMA ~

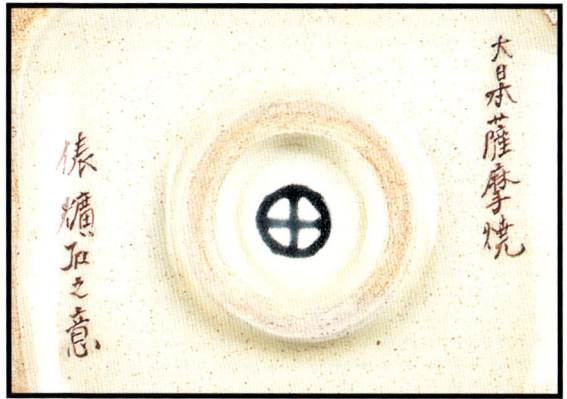

Mark of blue cross and two lines of red characters.

Kagoshima Satsuma figure of a standing woman holding a basket purse, 17" h. $5,635

Satsuma standing figure of a woman in dark blue robes with gold hem band holding a fan, 14.5" h.
Collection of Tom & Linda Tompkins

~ SATSUMA ~

Exceptionally large Satsuma figure of a
standing girl holding a scroll, 28.5" h. $14,490

~ SATSUMA ~

FIGURES OF MEN AND BOYS

Mark with 4 red characters.

Satsuma figure of a standing man with miter hat, holding a walking stick, 12.75" h. $4,025

~ SATSUMA ~

Satsuma figure of Hotei holding a bag and a gourd, 10" h. $4,830

Satsuma seated Hotei figure, 5.25" h. $2,415

~ SATSUMA ~

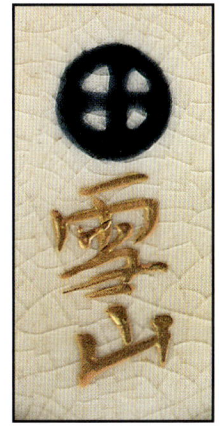

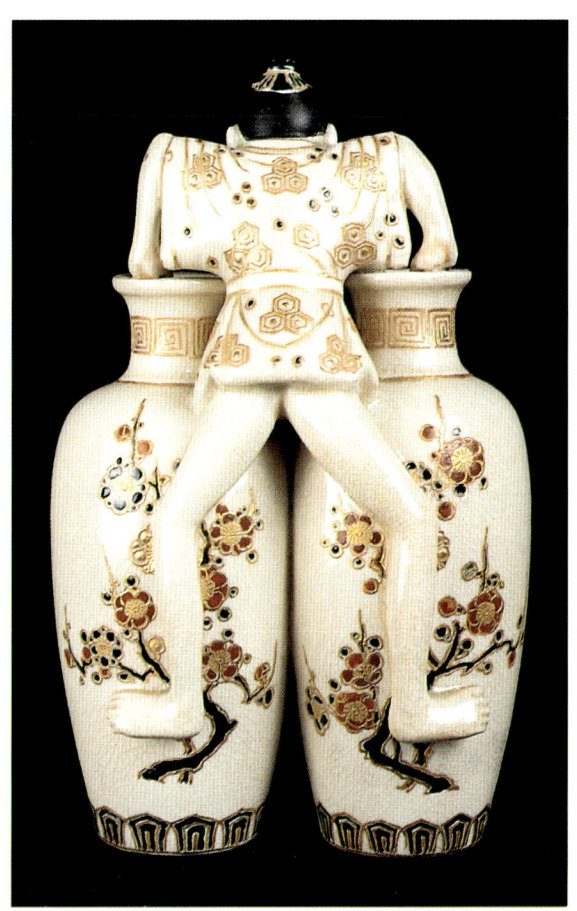

Satsuma double vase with two men figures, Ashenaga and Tenaga, 6.5" h.

~ 115 ~

~ SATSUMA ~

ANIMALS

Satsuma figure of a crouching dog with neck collar and ball, 6.5" h. $4,025

PLATES, ROUND

Satsuma plate painted with a monkey scratching his left arm, 12" l. $4,025

~ 116 ~

~ SATSUMA ~

Large Satsuma plate with decoration of two old men and young boy, c. 1860-1910, 12" d. $1,200

Satsuma bowl decorated with a large man with three children, c. 1860-1910, 9.75" d. $570

Large Satsuma dish decorated with nine scholars near water and hills, scalloped edge, c. 1860-1910, 15" d. $1,200

Large Satsuma bowl decorated with a scene of a man slaying a dragon, c. 1860-1910, 12" d. $800

~ SATSUMA ~

Satsuma dish decorated with man playing a stringed instrument, 9.25" d. *Collection of Tom & Linda Tompkins*

Satsuma plate of off-white color and finely painted decoration with gold depicting a Japanese building next to the sea with figures in the foreground and a spiral band of flowers at the top, marked. *Collection of Tom & Linda Tompkins*

~ 118 ~

~ SATSUMA ~

PLATES, SHAPED

Satsuma rectangular dish with floral decoration, 5.75" l. $1,290

Two similar Satsuma dishes of off-white color with oval bases and four scalloped lobes of fan shapes, 7" l. *Collection of Tom & Linda Tompkins*

~ 119 ~

~ SATSUMA ~

BOWLS

Right & below: Satsuma bowl decorated inside and outside with different scenes of people within variously shaped overlapping reserves, 5.5" d. $1,950

Scalloped Satsuma bowl decorated with old men, c. 1860-1910, 8.25" d. $570

~ SATSUMA ~

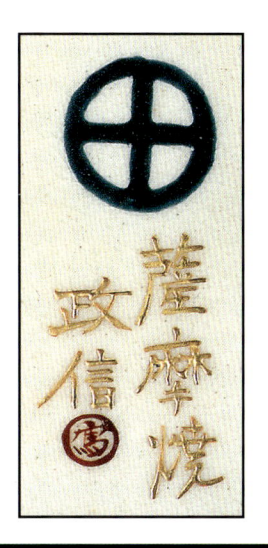

Satsuma bowl with floral and landscape decoration and scalloped rim. 7.5" d. $2,576

~ SATSUMA ~

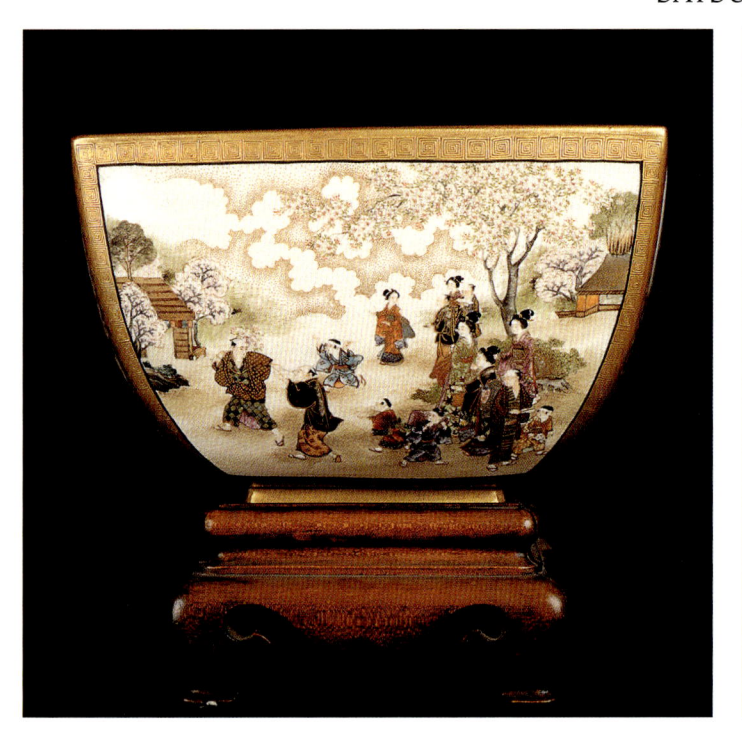

Square Satsuma bowl with four scenes of people in landscapes on the outside and floral blossoms surrounding a white dragon and clouds on the inside, marked by decorator Ryozan, 8" w. $8,050

~ 122 ~

~ SATSUMA ~

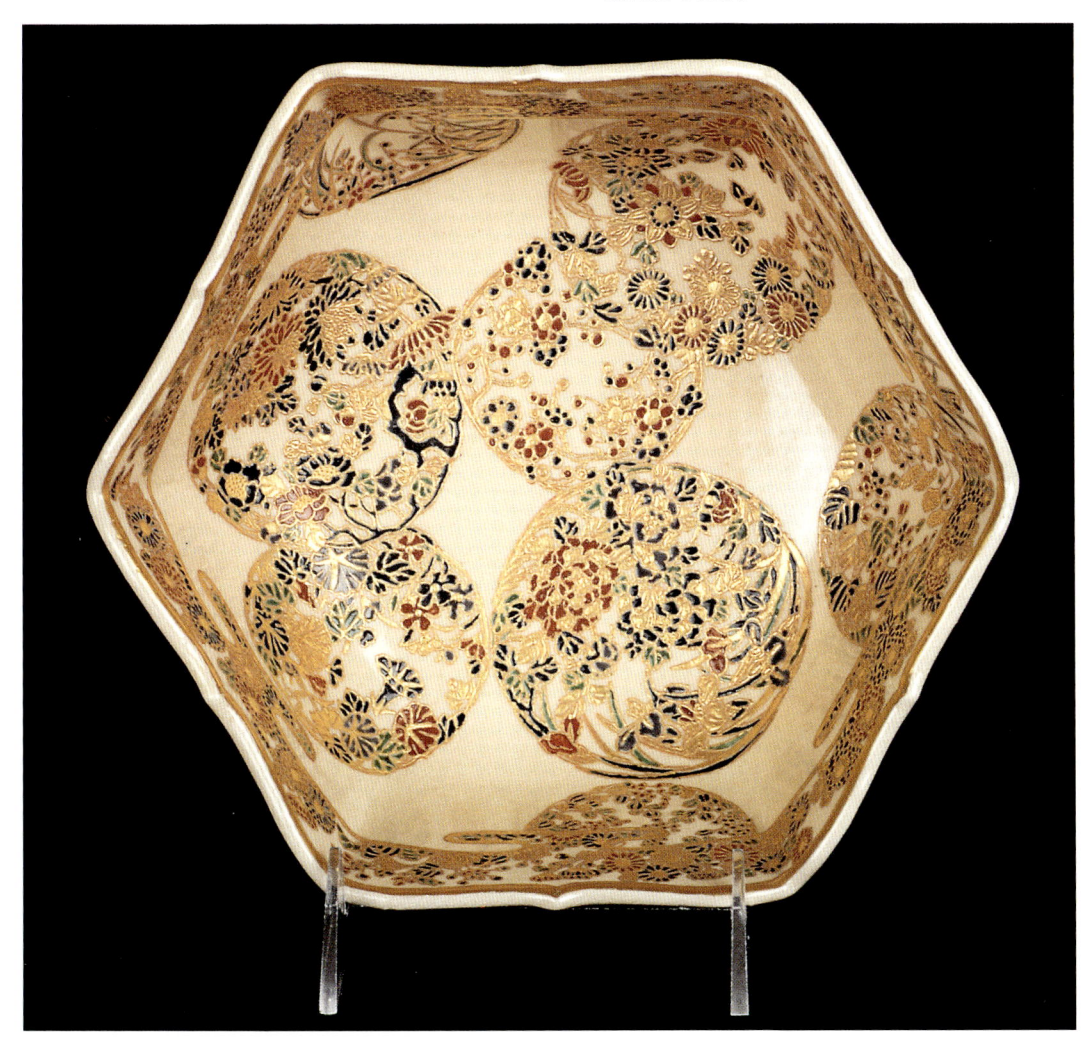

Satsuma six-sided bowl with circles of floral decorations and Imperial blue glaze, blue cross and gold marks along with an impressed mark, 8.5" d. $3,220-4,025

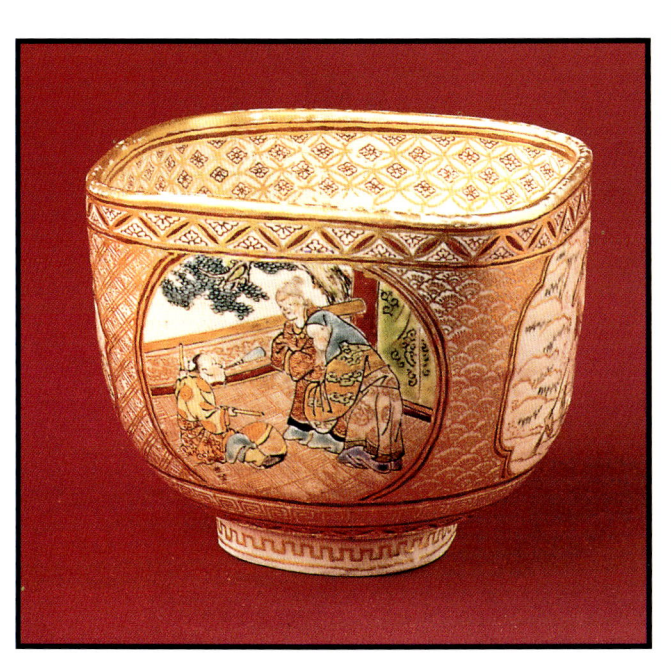

Small Satsuma square bowl with decorated panels, 3.25" h. *Collection of Tom & Linda Tompkins*

~ 123 ~

~ SATSUMA ~
BOTTLES

Pair of Satsuma flat flask vases covered with rectangular panels painted with scenes of people and floral designs, 7.25" h. $4,830

Pair of small Satsuma flat round flask vases with detailed scenes of many people gathered, 3" h. $4,830

~ SATSUMA ~

Top: Pair of Satsuma donut-shaped vases decorated on one side with birds in a garden setting and on the reverse with men of the martial arts, 4.75" h.

Bottom: Pair of early Satsuma bottles with blue leaf and green pine frond decoration, 9.5" h. *Collection of Tom & Linda Tompkins*

~ 125 ~

~ SATSUMA ~

Pair of Satsuma bottles with green glaze and band of relief chrysanthemum blossoms, by Tanzan, 7" h. *Collection of Tom & Linda Tompkins*

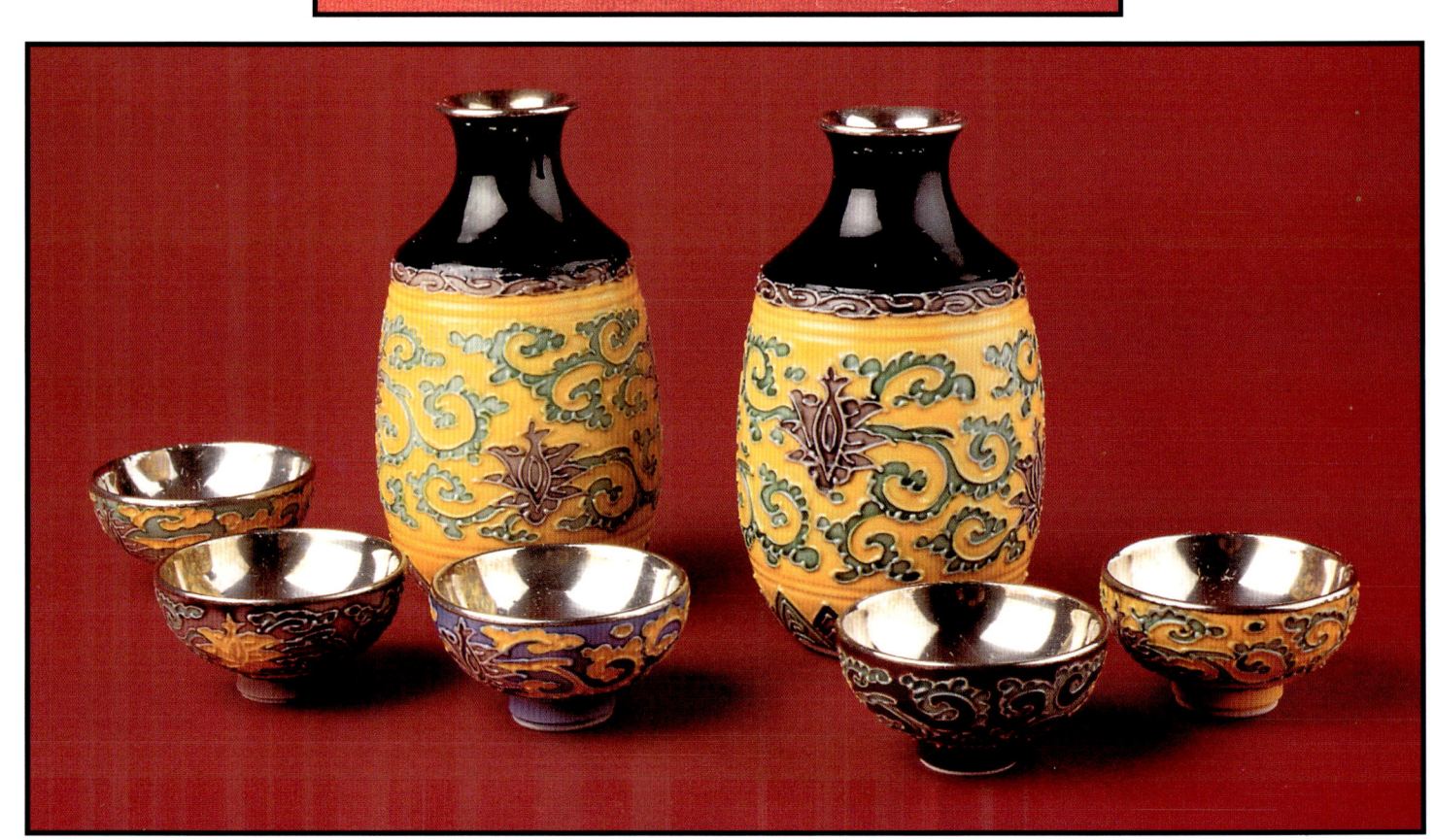

Pair of Satsuma saki bottles decorated with polychrome relief design by Zengoro Iraku with five saki cups, each lined with silver, 3.75" h. *Collection of Tom & Linda Tompkins*

~ SATSUMA ~

VASES WITH FLORAL DECORATION

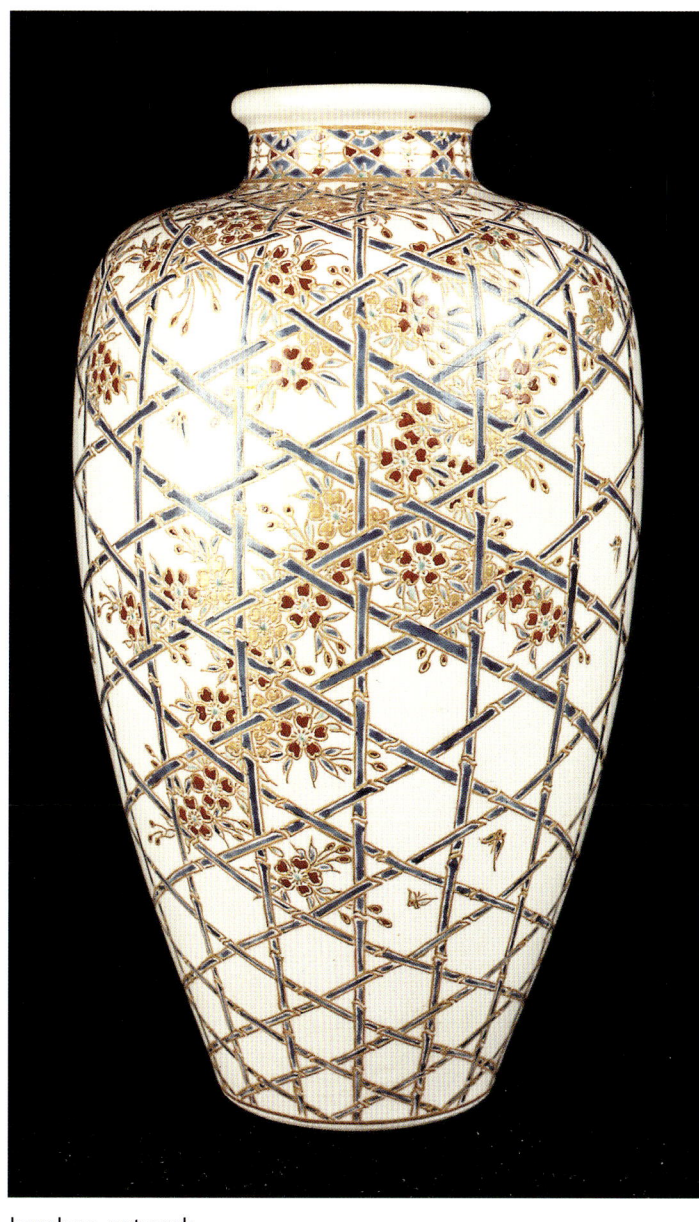

Satsuma vase with bamboo network and floral decoration, 8.75" h. $4,025

~ SATSUMA ~

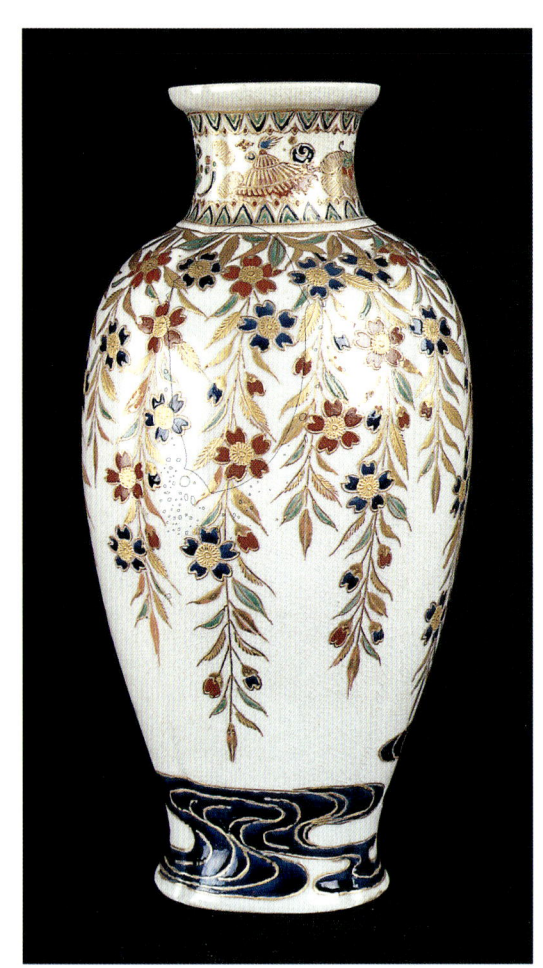

Top left: Satsuma ovoid vase with floral vine decoration, 9.5" h. $3,220

Bottom right: Large Kagoshima Satsuma vase with white background and three friends decoration of pine, plum blossoms and bamboo, early 19th century, four-character Satsuma mark with blue cross, 18.5" h. $10,465-11,270

~ SATSUMA ~

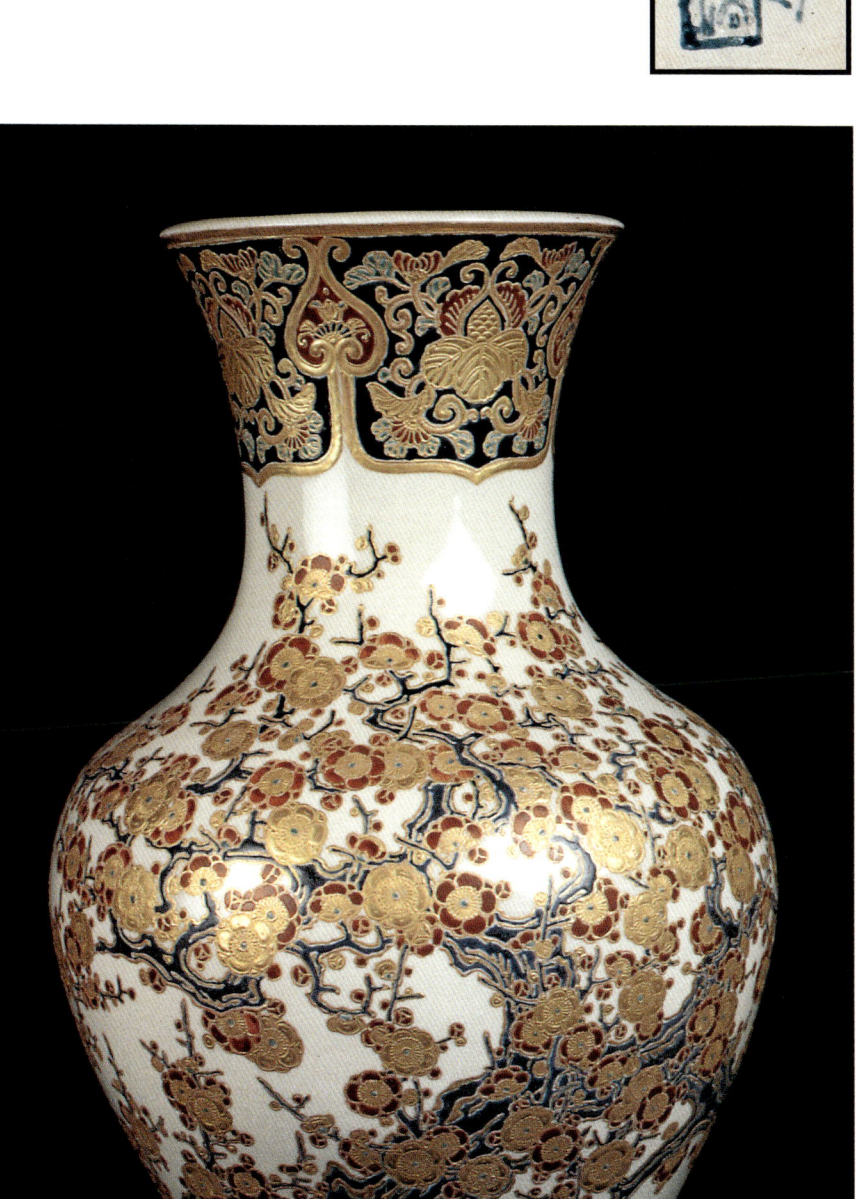

Top right: Satsuma vase with dragon and floral decoration, Imperial Gozu blue glaze, 12.5" h. $8,050

Bottom left: Satsuma vase with plum blossom decoration, gold marks and red square mark of Kinkozan, c. 1880, 12.25" h. $19,320

~ SATSUMA ~

Top left: Pair of Satsuma vases with floral decoration, 7" h. $4,830

Bottom left: Satsuma double gourd vase with chrysanthemum decoration, 9.5" h. $4,830

Bottom center: Mark against a heavy crackle background.

~ 130 ~

~ SATSUMA ~

Top left: Early Satsuma vase with dark blue surface and white scrolls, unmarked, 12.25" h. $4,830

Top & bottom right: Satsuma Kagoshima vase with red background and blue bamboo decoration, 19" high. *Collection of Tom & Linda Tompkins*

~ 131 ~

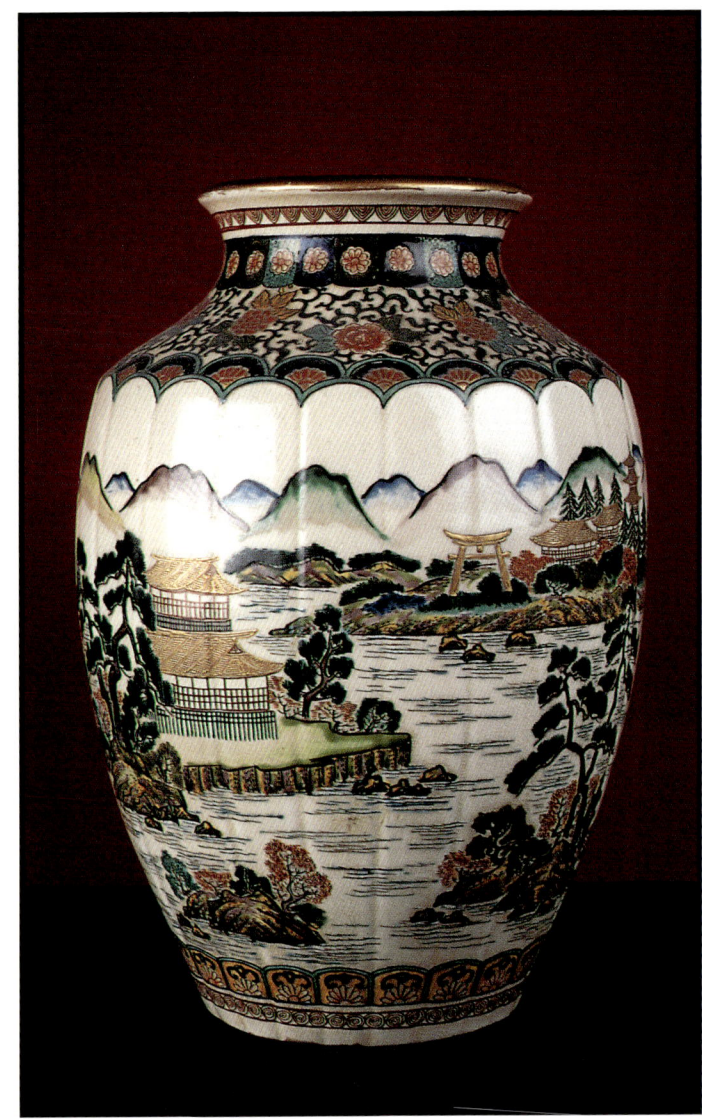

~ SATSUMA ~

Satsuma vase with ribbed sides and landscape decoration, c. 1860-1910, 12" h.

Two miniature Satsuma vases with floral decoration: bottle shape, 4" h.; urn shape, 4" h. *Collection of Tom & Linda Tompkins*

Pair of old Satsuma vases with Gosu blue decoration and off-white background, overglaze polychrome floral decoration, 9.4" h. *Collection of Tom & Linda Tompkins*

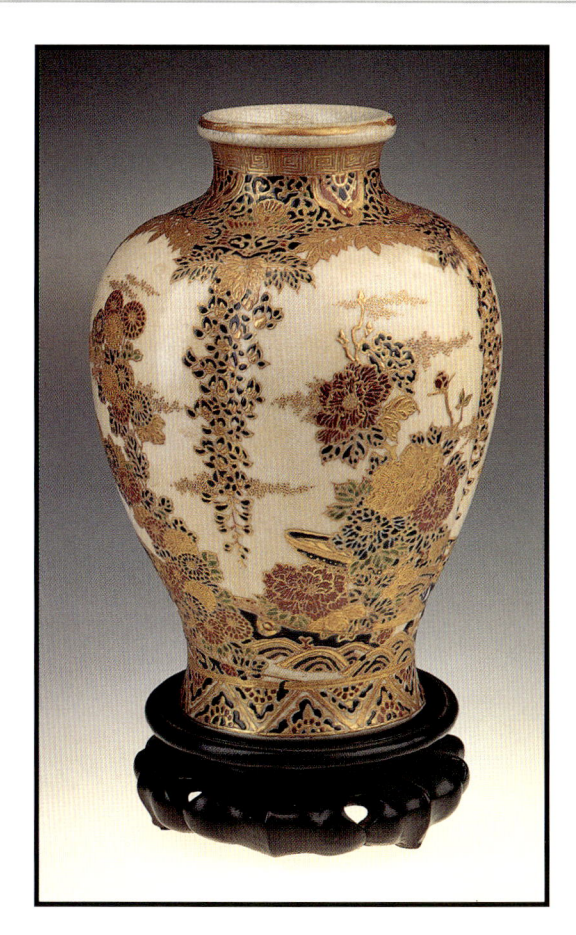

~ SATSUMA ~

Top left: : Satsuma vase. *Courtesy of Bruce Waters*

Bottom left: Old Satsuma vase with dark off-white background and side handles picked out in gold on a red ground, sides decorated with tapestry bands, 4" h. *Collection of Tom & Linda Tompkins*

Large Satsuma vase with ring side handles and polychrome floral decoration, 33" h. *Collection of Tom & Linda Tompkins*

~ 133 ~

~ SATSUMA ~

VASES WITH PEOPLE DECORATION

Pair of Satsuma vases with Imperial Gosu blue glaze and many people in the decoration in mirror images, blue cross and two gold marks, 11.5" h. $14,490

~ SATSUMA ~

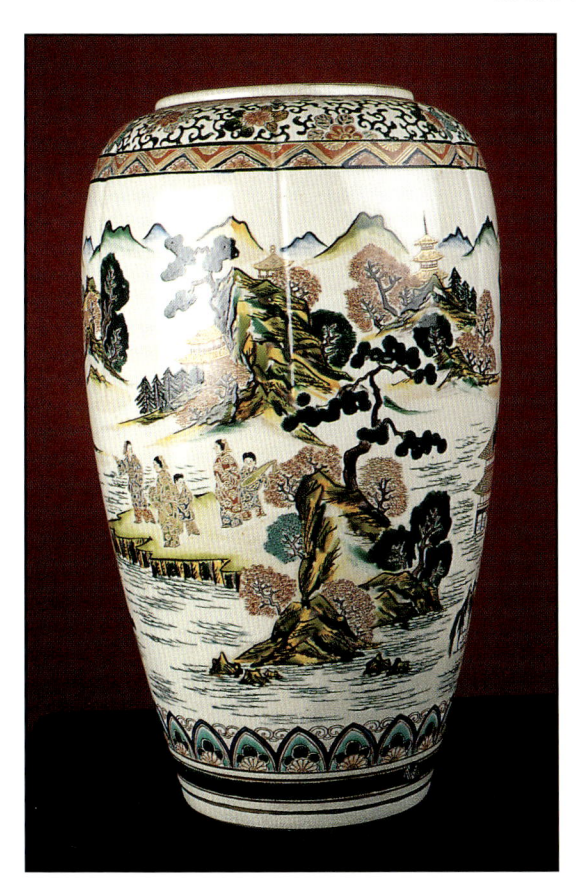

Top left: Satsuma ovoid vase with water landscape decoration, c. 1860-1910, 12.75" h.

Bottom: Pair of fine quality Satsuma vases with grisaille landscape decoration on one side and polychrome scenes of four men on the other side, silver and gold pierced work at the rims, c. 1870, 9.5" h. $7,245

~ SATSUMA ~

Pair of large Satsuma vases, each decorated in fine detail with four scenes of men and women, c.1870, 19.25" h. $8,050

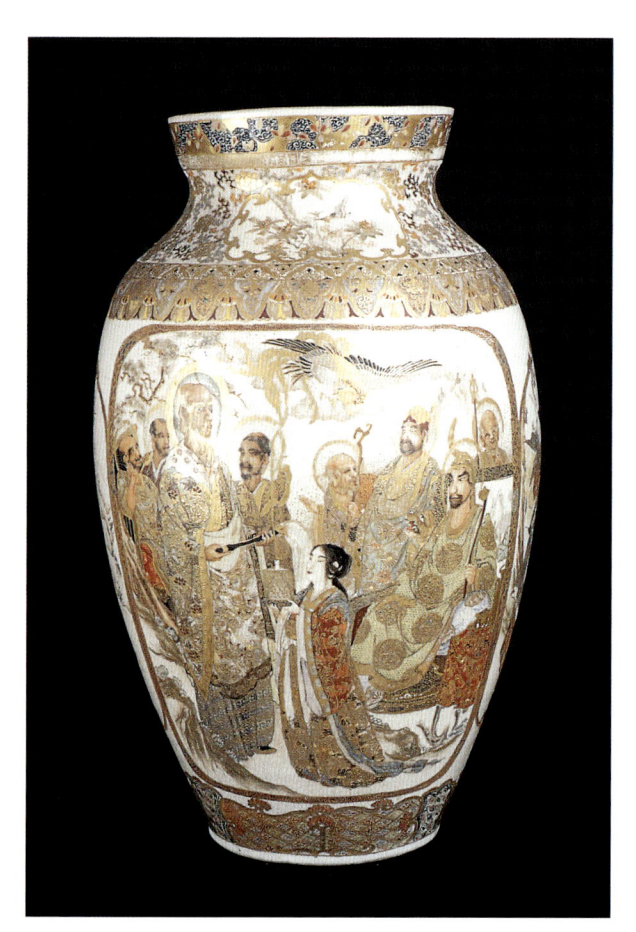

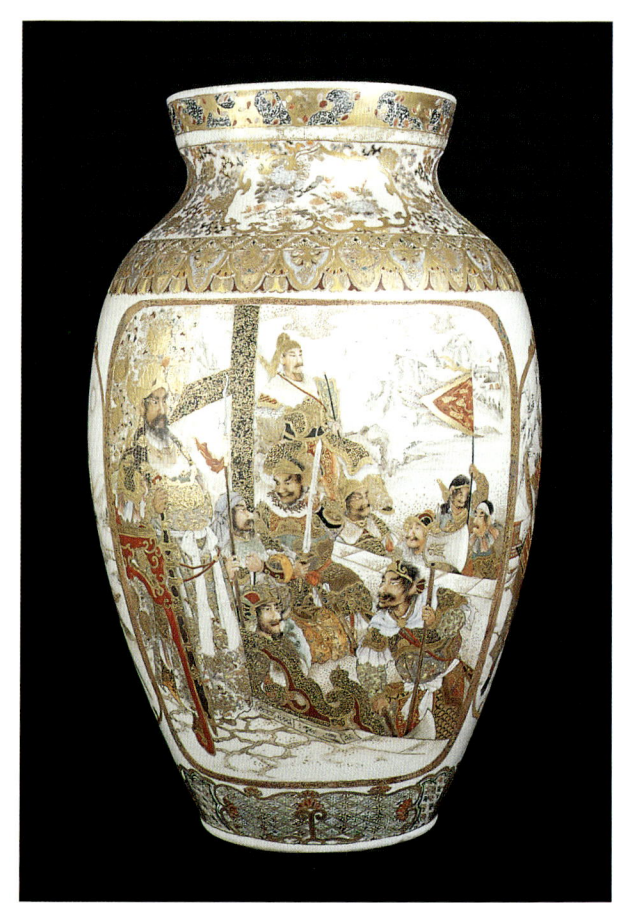

~ SATSUMA ~

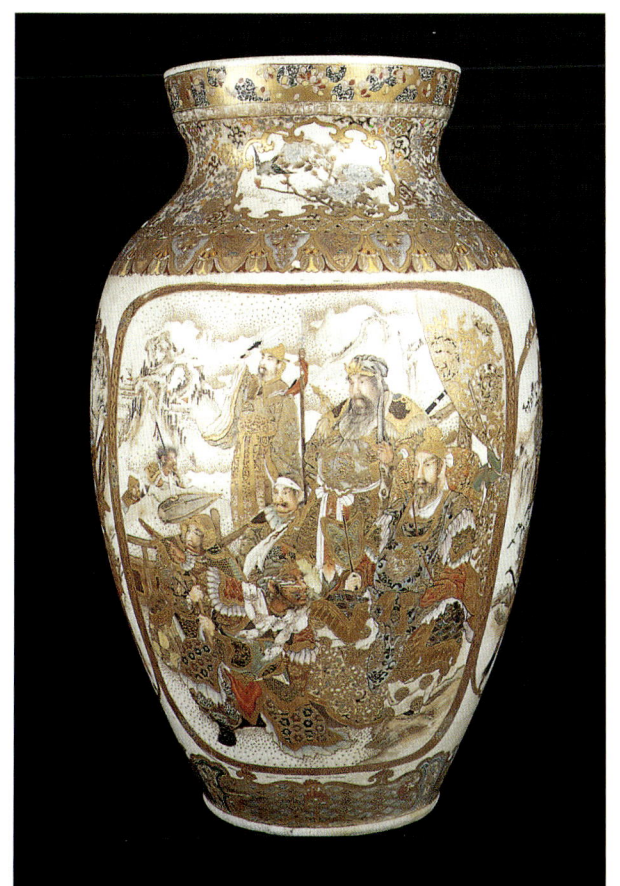

~ 137 ~

~ SATSUMA ~

Pair of tall Satsuma vases with raised gold work at the rims and each with different scenes of two men and two women, c. 1870, 23.75" h. Pair $10,465

SATSUMA

~ SATSUMA ~

Top right: Pair of Satsuma vases with groups of men, women and children, and family in landscapes, c. 1860-1910, 12.5" h. $1,290

Left: Pair of Satsuma vases with decoration of a single warrior in a winter landscape, c. 1860-1910, 16" h. $2,900

Bottom right: Pair of Satsuma vases decorated with men and a large bird, c. 1860-1910, 18.25" h. $1,600

~ SATSUMA ~

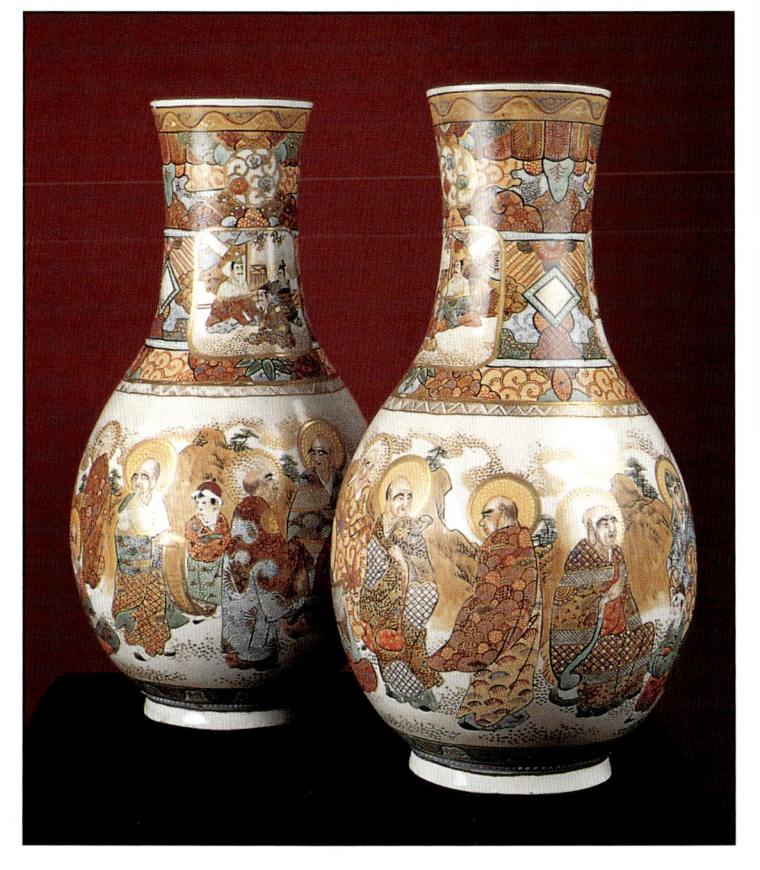

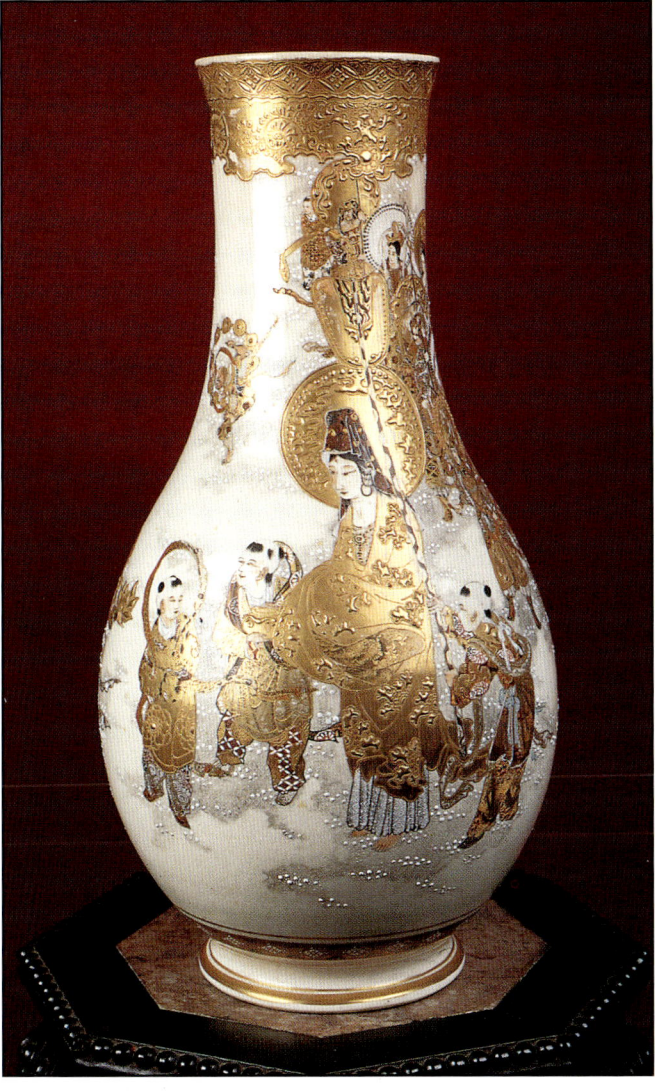

Top left: Pair of Satsuma urn-shaped vases painted with scenes of men in front of draped textiles and white flowers with butterflies, 6" h. $1,450

Bottom left: Pair of Satsuma bottle-shaped vases decorated with scholars, c. 1860-1910, 14.25" h. $1,125

Top right: Satsuma bottle-shaped vase showing a procession of people and children, c. 1860-1910, 18" h. $1,12

~ 141 ~

~ SATSUMA ~

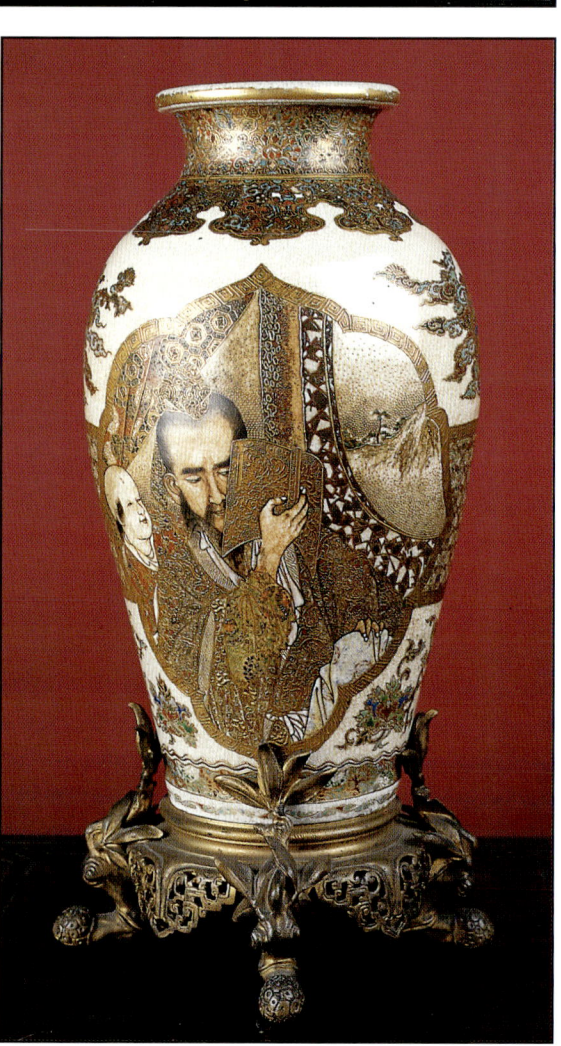

Top left: Pair of Satsuma vases with gold dot background and decoration of scholars, c. 1860-1910, 16" h. $2,737

Bottom left: Single vase decorated with painting of a single man with a book, c. 1860-1910, 11.5" h. and separate European ormolu base. $1,950

Bottom right: Satsuma vase with panels of Samurai decoration, c. 1860-1910, 14.75" h. $2,254

~ SATSUMA ~

Top left & right: : Pair of quality Satsuma vases painted with portraits of a man and a woman among intricate gold scroll and floral decorations, 9.25" h. Pair $2,900

Bottom right: Pair of Satsuma vases with Samurai and scholars, c. 1860-1910, 12" h. $975

~ SATSUMA ~

Pair of square Satsuma vases with two groups of men in the decoration and square rims, c. 1860-1910, 12" h. $1,450

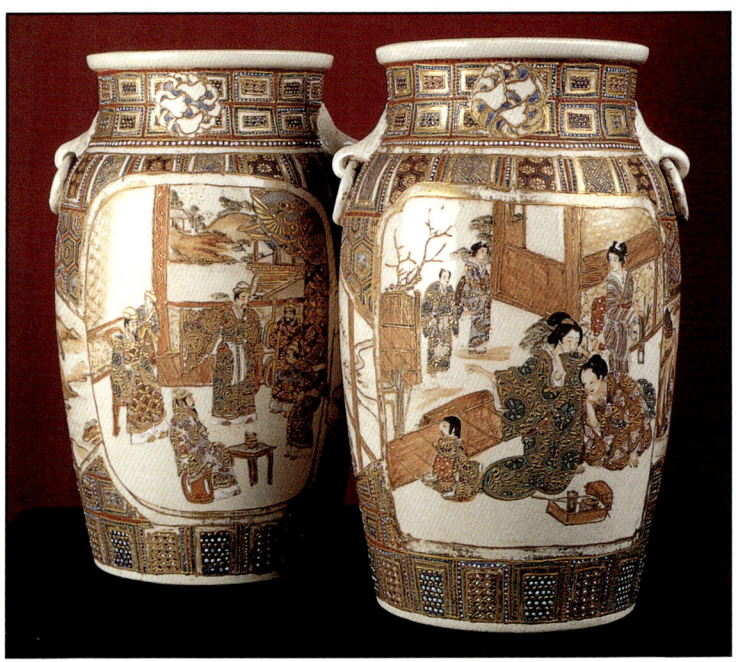

Pair of round Satsuma vases with white ring handles and decoration of people in room interiors, c. 1860-1910, 9.75" h. $1,370

Pair of Satsuma straight sided vases with panels of musicians and dancers, c. 1860-1910, 12.25" h.

~ SATSUMA ~

Top: Pair of Satsuma vases decorated with men and children scenes, c. 1860-1910, 12" h. and with added European ormolu rims and bases. $2,250

Bottom left: Pair of Satsuma vases with painted scenes of a woman and a child and with two men with books, c. 1860-1910, 12.25" h. $1,290

Bottom right: Pair of Satsuma vases with Samurai and scholars, c. 1860-1910, 12" h. $1,450

~ SATSUMA ~

Top right: Pair of Satsuma vases with Samurai and children panels, c. 1860-1910, 18" h. $4,500

Bottom left & right: : Pair of bulbous Satsuma vases showing gods and Confucius, c. 1860-1910, 9.75" h. $4,025

~ SATSUMA ~

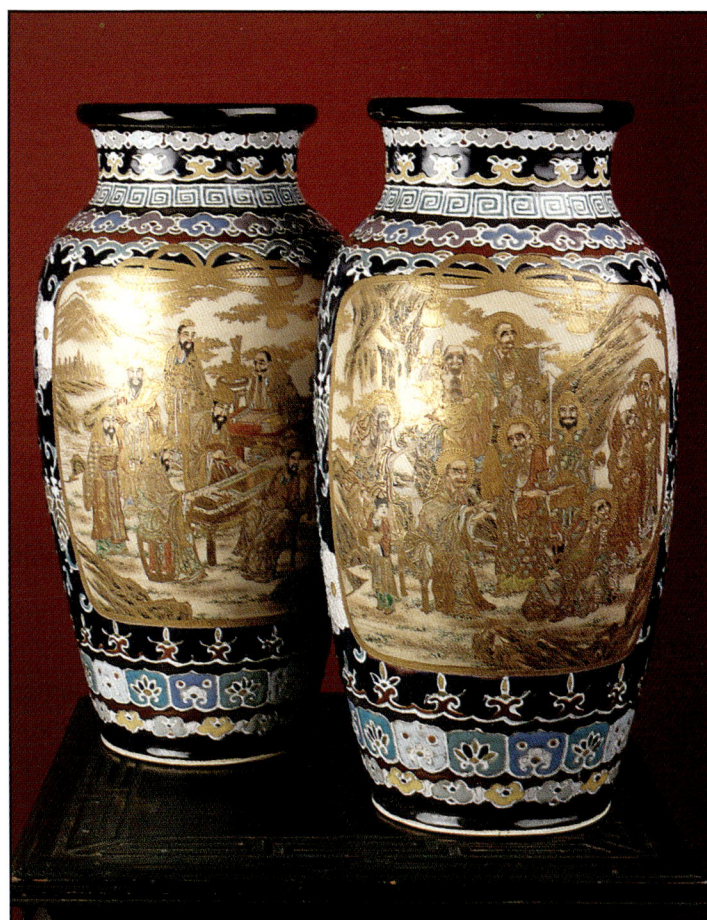

Top left: Pair of straight-sided Satsuma vases with scenes of Samurai and family, c. 1860-1910, 12" h. mounted on European ormolu bases. $2,900

Top right: Pair of Satsuma vases with gold scenes of men surrounded by a cord tied at the top in a bow and polychrome thick floral glazes, c. 1860-1910, 15.5" h.

Bottom left: Pair of Satsuma vases with painted decoration of child, father and grandfather in garden and Samurai scenes, c. 1860-1910, 18" h. $2,750

~ SATSUMA ~

Top: Pair of Satsuma vases with red details and landscape scenes with people, c. 1860-1910, 12" h. $1,130

Bottom left: Satsuma vase. *Courtesy of Bruce Waters*

Bottom right: Satsuma vase. *Courtesy of Bruce Waters*

~ SATSUMA ~

Top left: Pair of Satsuma vases with Samurai and women with children decoration, c. 1860-1910, 9.5" h.

Top right: Pair of Satsuma vases showing scholars teaching a youth and Samurai and floral background, c. 1860-1910, 12" h. $1,775

Bottom: Pair of Satsuma vases showing scholars teaching a youth and Samurai warriors c.1860-1910, 12" h. $1,290

~ SATSUMA ~

Top: Pair of Satsuma ovoid vases decorated with scenes of men in garden and landscape setting, c. 1860-1910, 17.75" h. $4,500

Bottom left: Single Satsuma vase with decoration of a woman and child, c. 1860-1910, 18.5" h. $2,750

Bottom right: One of a pair of Satsuma vases with red and black floral decoration and scholars in landscape decoration, c. 1860-1910, 25" h. $2,254

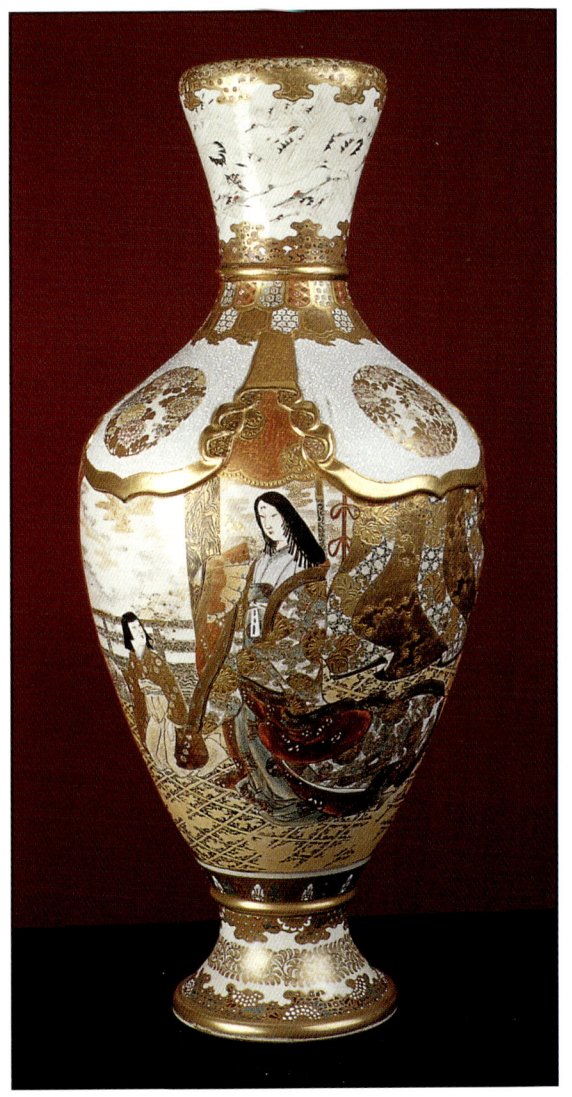

SATSUMA

Satsuma vase with Samurai decoration mounted as an electric lamp, vase 18" h. c. 1860-1910, $1,290

Satsuma vase with two panels of scholars teaching a youth. Top edge repaired with staples, c. 1860-1910, 21.25" h. $885

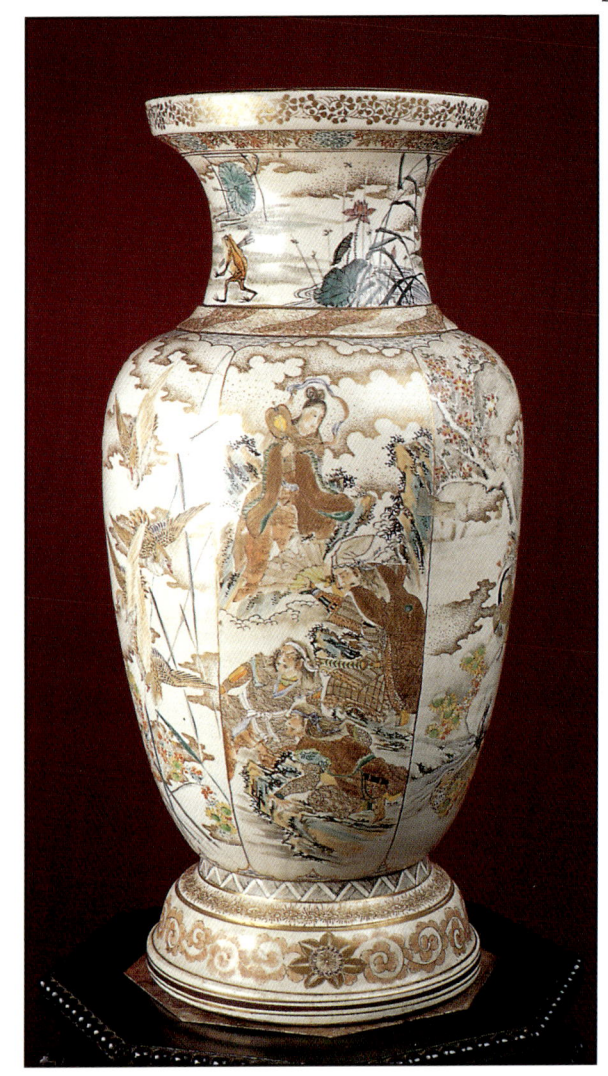

~ SATSUMA ~

Top left: Satsuma vase decorated with alternating panels of Samurai warriors and birds in a garden designs, top band with frogs as archers, c. 1860-1910, 20.5" h. $2,420

Bottom left: Pair of Satsuma vases with central band showing a procession of people in water, c. 1860-1910, 12" h. $1,130

Bottom right: Pair of Satsuma vases with scenes of scholars and youth, c. 1860-1910, 19" h. $2,900

~ SATSUMA ~

Top: Pair of Satsuma six-sided vases decorated with many rectangles of painted people and flowers, c. 1860-1910, 7.25" h. $725

Bottom left: Large Satsuma vase with two ring handles and decoration of fish and water spirits, c. 1860-1910, 15.25" h. $725

Bottom right: Satsuma vase with relief dragon and groups of saints and scholars, c. 1860-1910, 8.5" h. $245

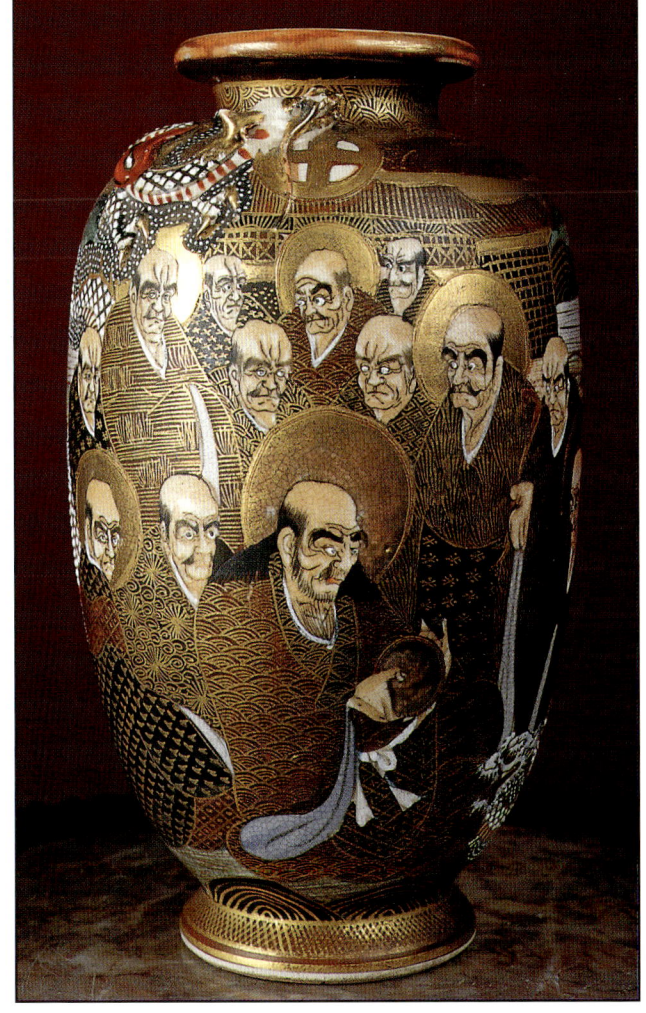

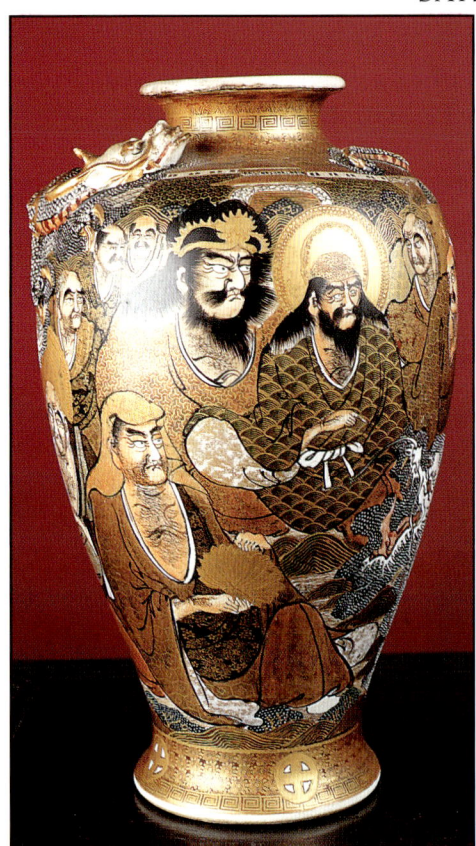

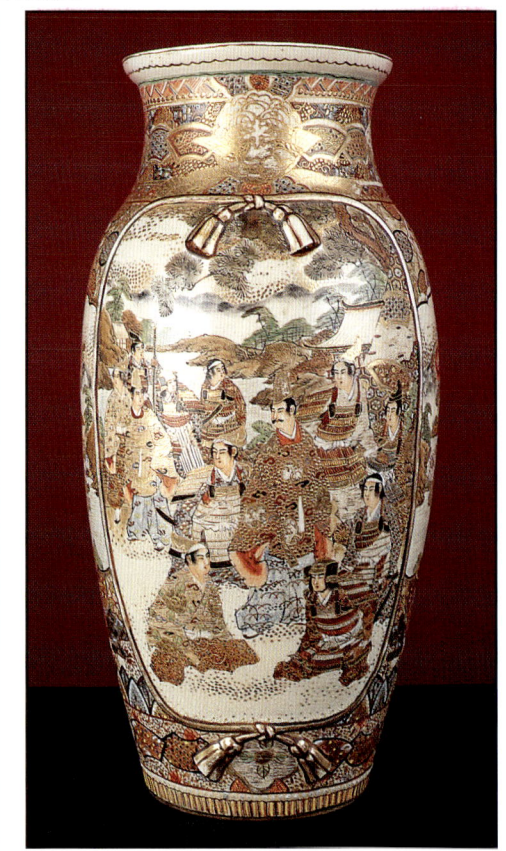

~ SATSUMA ~

Top left: Satsuma vase with relief dragon and painted scholars decoration, c. 1860-1910, 12.5" h. $810

Top right: Satsuma vase with bow-tied frame around panels of Samurai and a family, c. 1860-1910, 14.25" h.

Bottom: Pair of Satsuma vases with bow-tied panel borders around scenes of Samurai warriors and family groups, floral background. c. 1860-1910, 12" h. $1,130

~ 154 ~

SATSUMA

Satsuma vase with people in landscapes in panels with a bow-tied rope at the top and bird decoration, c. 1860-1910, 24" h. $1,290

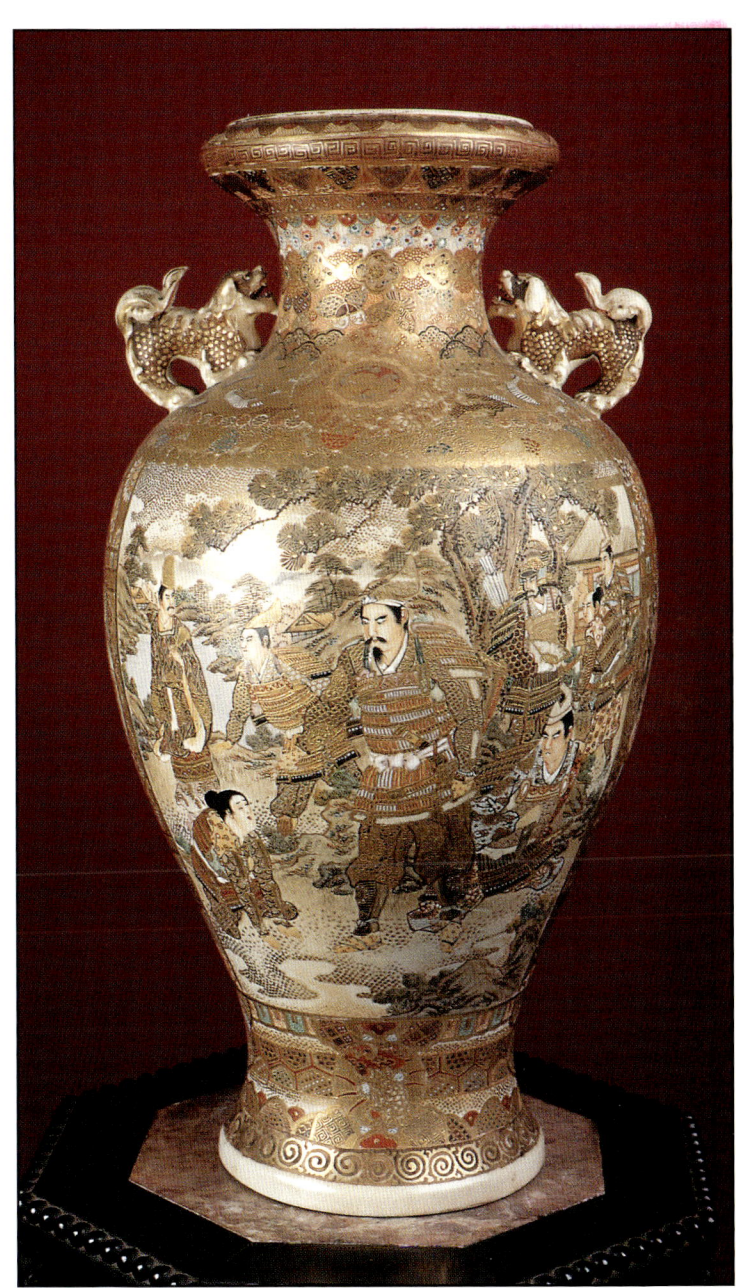

Large Satsuma vase with lion dog handles, a Tokugawa crest, and Samurai decoration, c. 1860-1910, 18.5" h. $1,950

~ SATSUMA ~

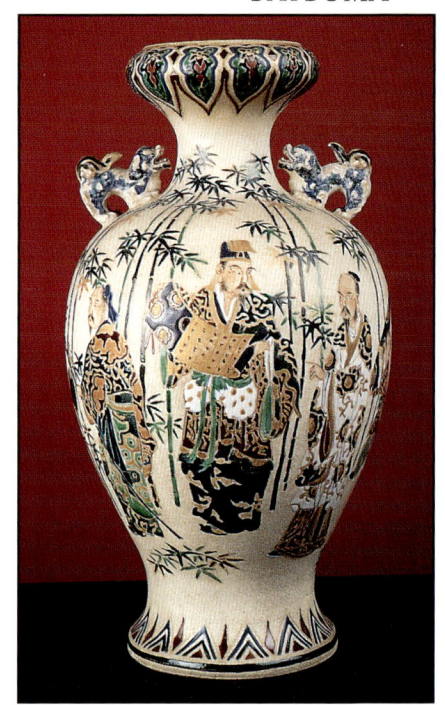

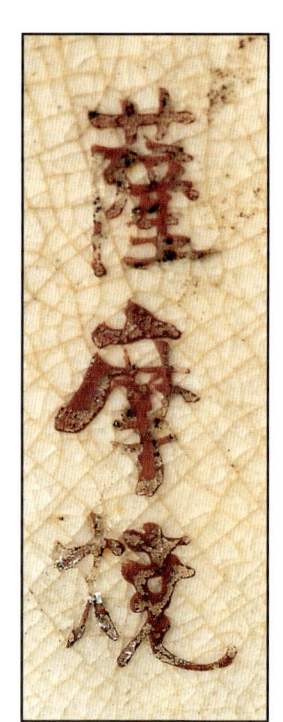

Top: Satsuma vase with blue foo dog side handles and decoration of scholars in a bamboo grove, c. 1860-1910, 12.25" h. $1,450

Bottom: Pair of Satsuma vases with gold background and crowd of people, side handles, c. 1860-1910, 12.3" h. $1,950

~ SATSUMA ~

Top: Pair of Satsuma vases with gold foo dog handles and scenes of people in a landscape and Samurai, c. 1860-1910, 12" h. $2,415

Bottom left: Pair of Satsuma vases decorated with gold dragon side handles and painted scene with women and children and with a family group, c. 1860-1910, 11.75" h. $1,930

Bottom right: Pair of Satsuma vases with lion mask handles and decoration of Samurai and of women fishing with children, c. 1860-1910, 12" h. $800

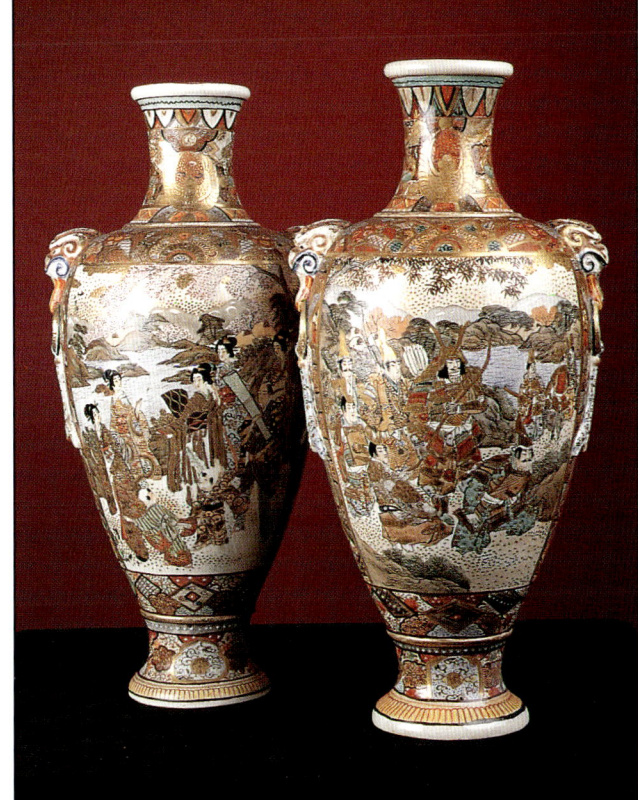

~ 157 ~

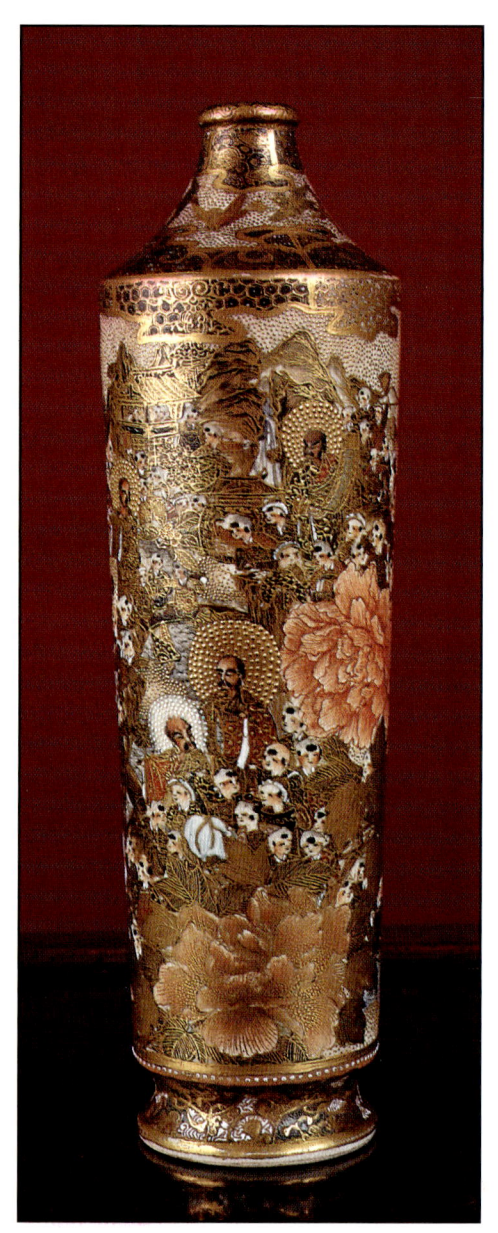

~ SATSUMA ~

Pair of small Satsuma square bottle vases with scenes of people in landscapes, 3.5" h. $2,900

Tall and thin round bottle vase decorated with "thousand faces" decoration, 7.25" h. $1,932

Pair of Satsuma foo dog figures supporting vases on their backs, 7.5" h. $1,625

~ SATSUMA ~

Top left: Pair of vases with flaring rims decorated in brown with many faces, c. 1860-1910, 17.5" h. $1,930

Top right: Satsuma tall necked vase with elaborate gold and red decoration including people in a landscape, children, and group of men, c. 1860-1910, 17.25" h. $975

Bottom: Pair of Satsuma double gourd vases with scenes of people in landscapes, 6.25" h. $1,370

~ 159 ~

~ SATSUMA ~

Pair of tall bottle vases with blue background interrupted by painted balls and gold flowers, c. 1860-1910, 16.5" h. $650

Pair of double gourd vases with relief dragon and brown men decoration, c. 1860-1910, 11" h. $1,290

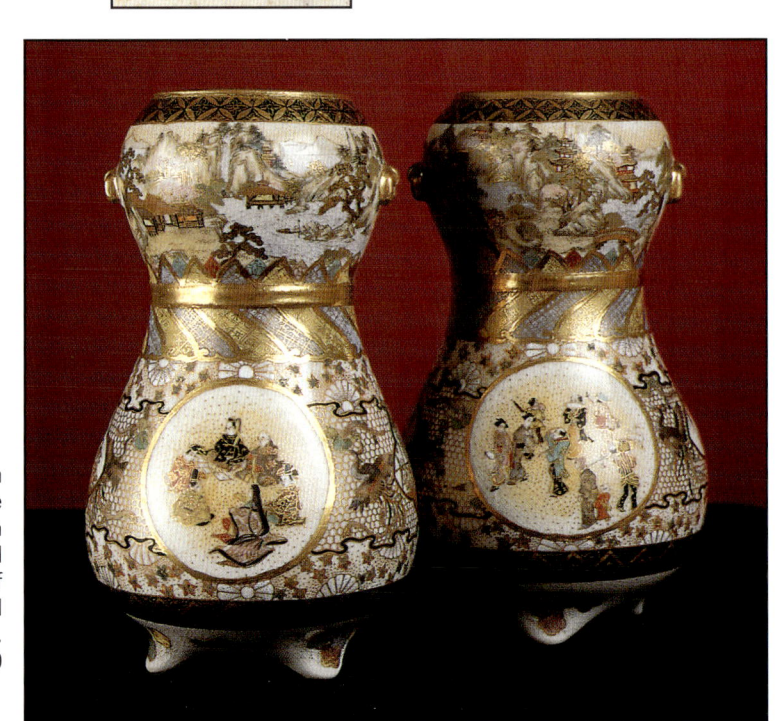

Pair of Satsuma vases of double gourd shape on feet decorated with reserves of people and floral landscapes, 4.8" h. $1,950

~ 160 ~

~ SATSUMA ~

Top: Pair of Satsuma vases with bands of decoration including children playing in a landscape, c. 1860-1910, 18.5" h. $4,025

Bottom left: Pair of Satsuma round vases with dark blue background and panels of women in landscape and Samurai decoration, c. 1860-1910, 10.5" h. $1,950

Bottom right: Pair of Satsuma six-sided vases with thousand faces decoration c. 1860-1910, 7.25" h. $1,125

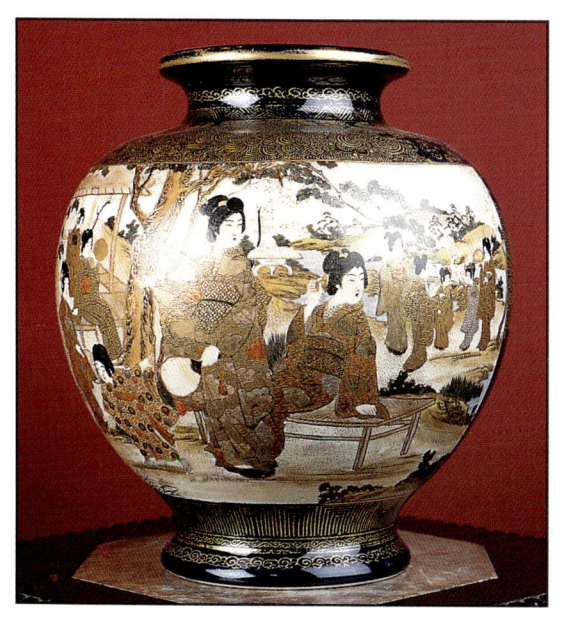

~ SATSUMA ~

VASES WITH BIRDS AND ANIMALS DECORATION

Large Satsuma vase painted with flying geese decoration, c. 1860-1910, 42.5" h.

~ SATSUMA ~

Single Satsuma vase of thin shape with yellow background and quail decoration, signed on the bottom, c. 1860-1910, 11" h.

Satsuma vase of bird shape with Imperial blue glaze, a shape derived from an archaic Chinese bronze, 5.75" h. $4,025

~ SATSUMA ~

Large Satsuma vase with exceedingly detailed painted decoration of many different birds among trees and flowers, three feet, and two scrolled handles, early 19th century, 18" h. $19,320

~ SATSUMA ~

~ SATSUMA ~

Satsuma vase decorated with six lions playing with tapestry balls and ribbons on a white ground, marked, 8.25" h. $4,830

~ SATSUMA ~

JARS

Top: Pair of covered jars on three white elephant-head feet, three scenes of the stages of a boy's life: as a child, warrior, and father, with seated lion finials, c. 1860-1910, 12" h. $1,290

Bottom: Large Satsuma lidded jar with gold lion finial and handles, and decoration of men in a garden and Samurai warriors, c. 1860-1910, 17" h. $975

~ SATSUMA ~

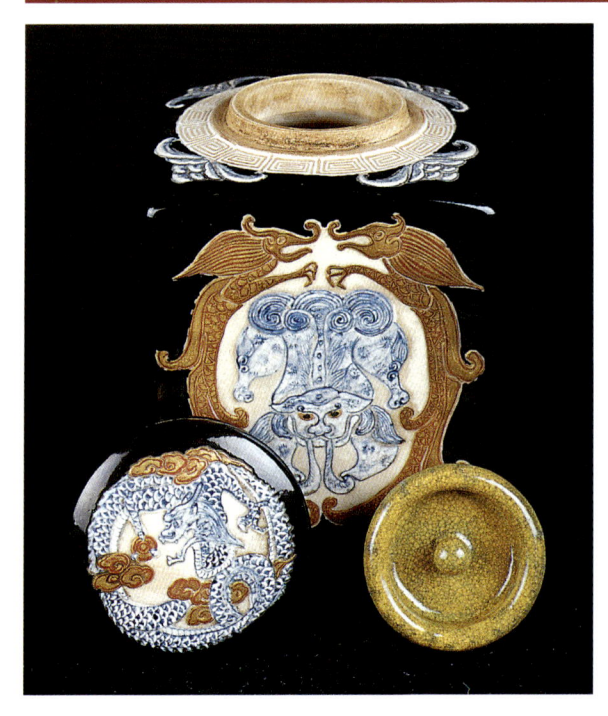

Satsuma tea caddie with square body and two-part lid, 5.75" h. $2,415

~ 168 ~

~ SATSUMA ~

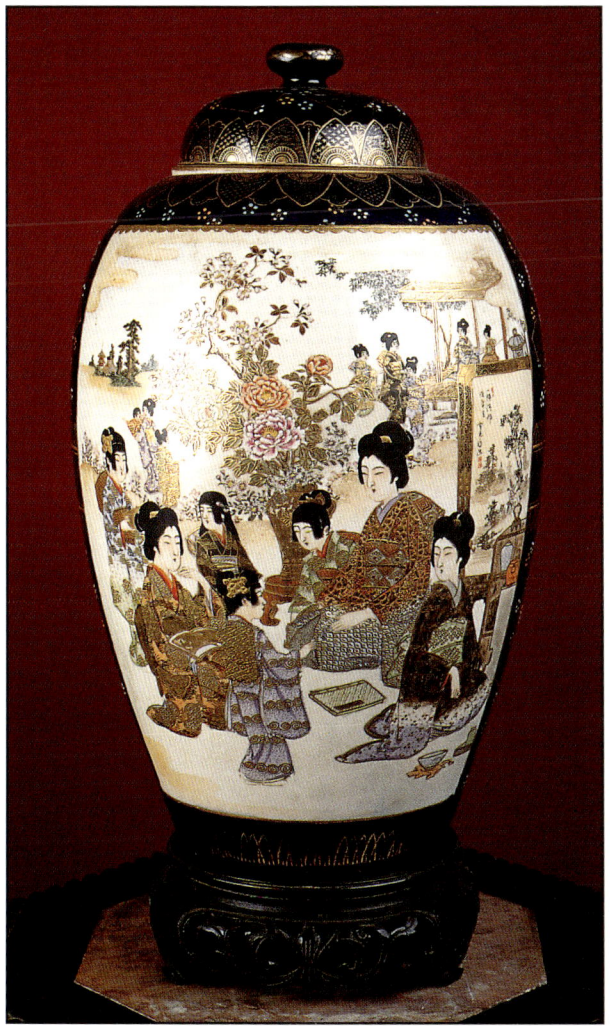

Top: Satsuma covered round bowl with pierced lid and two dark blue snake-form side handles and Imperial blue glaze, 3.25" h. $4,025

Bottom left: Satsuma covered jar with dark blue background and panels decorated with saints in landscape and women in a garden, c. 1860-1910, 15" h.

Bottom right: Globular Satsuma bowl with floral decoration including Imperial blue glaze and pierced silver lid, 3.5" h. $3,220-4,025

~ SATSUMA ~

SPECIALTY SHAPES

~ SATSUMA ~

Extremely large Satsuma *koro* (incense burner) of intricate design and fine quality decoration including Imperial Gosu blue glaze, 19.5" h. $22,540

~ SATSUMA ~

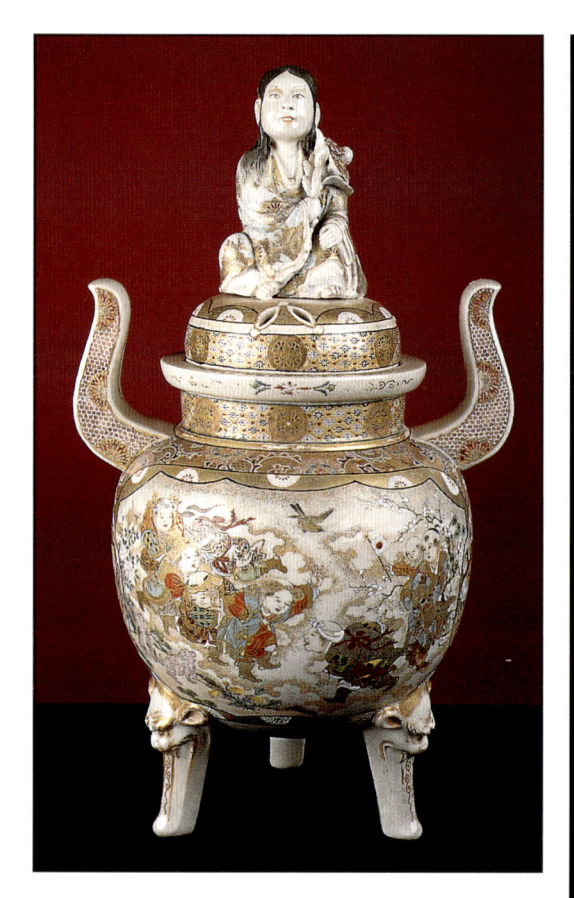

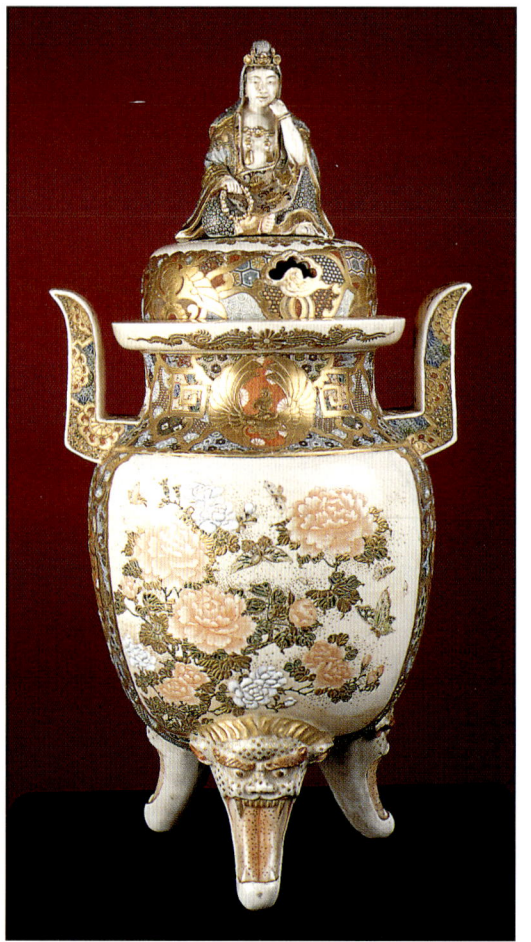

Top left: Satsuma *koro* with large seated figure as finial, and scenes of children playing a game and Samurai, c. 1860-1910, 16.5" h. $2,900

Bottom left: Large *koro* with floral and scholars decoration, seated figure as the finial, c. 1860-1910, 20.25" h. $3,220

Top right: Extremely large Satsuma *koro* on three legs with lion masks and scenes of room interiors with domestic activities, c. 1880, 25" h. $13,685

~ SATSUMA ~

Top left: Large *koro* with lion finial and three paw feet, decorated with people, c. 1860-1910, 18" h. $3,220

Top & bottom right: Large Satsuma *koro* with decorated panels of women and dragon and of a man and boy, c. 1860-1910, 23" h. $4,500

~ SATSUMA ~

Top: Satsuma *koro* with six side panels of Samurai figures in landscapes, pierced and repaired lid with large foo dog finial, c. 1860-1910, 19" h. $975

Bottom right: Satsuma incense burner in three sections: elephant-shaped base, decorated bowl, and pierced lid; gold decoration with polychrome details, 18" h. *Collection of Tom & Linda Tompkins*

~ SATSUMA ~

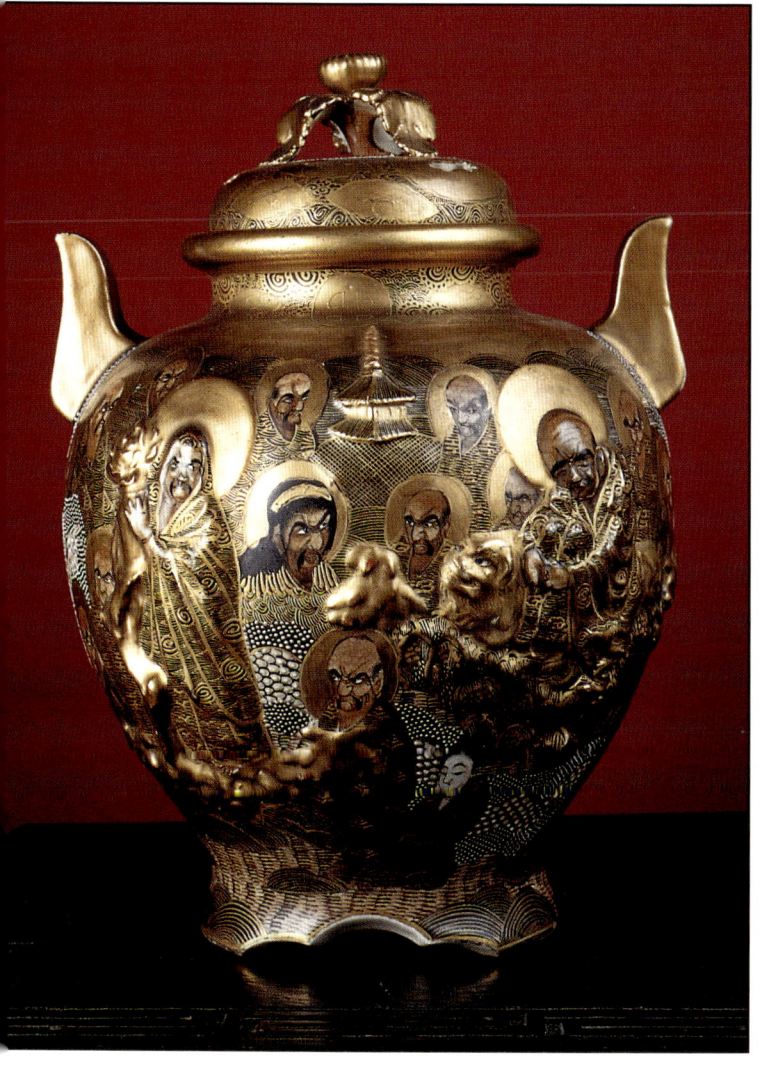

Top: Satsuma six-sided *koro* with side handles and piorood lid, 3.75" w. $1,450

Bottom left: Satsuma *koro* with gold background and many faces relief and painted decoration, c. 1860-1910, 12.5" h. $1,050

Bottom right: Satsuma teapot with dark blue background and panels decorated with three men and seated Samurai, c. 1860-1910, 6.5" h. $160

~ SATSUMA ~

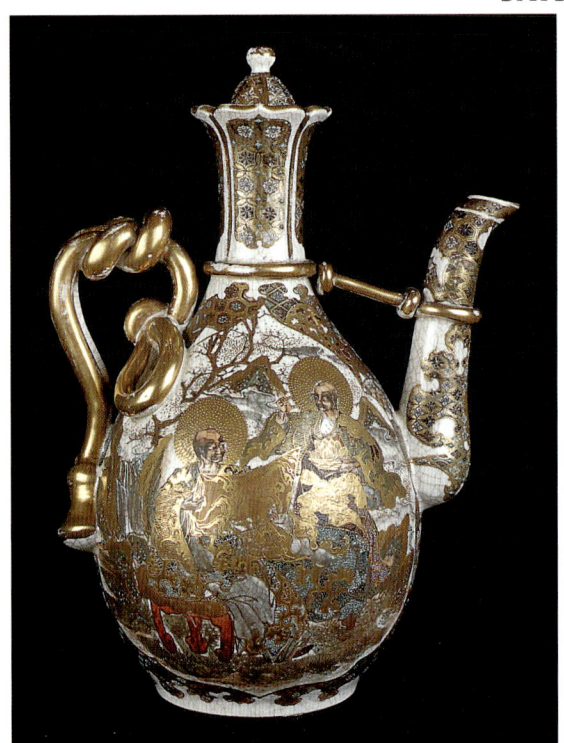

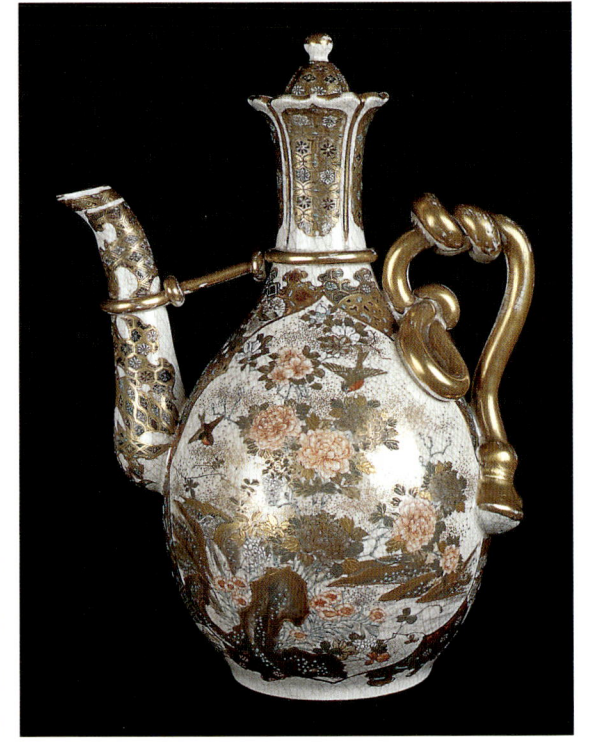

Top: Satsuma ewer with scholars and landscape decoration, a knotted rope handle, 11.25" h. $2,900

Bottom: Satsuma ewer with overall gold decoration including a multitude of faces and a boating scene, dragon spout, 10.25" h. $5,635

DECORATORS OF SATSUMA EARTHENWARE

It is interesting to isolate the work of late nineteenth century Satsuma decorators who signed their work and are recognized today. Many of these artists experimented with different decorating styles and even branched out to porcelain as well as earthenware shapes. They competed for recognition at the International Exhibitions in the late nineteenth century with the new "antique style" Satsuma and usually marked their pieces. Low production studio pieces are valued greatly today in the marketplace. The following few artist-decorators are leading figures in the Satsuma market today.

Kinkozan

Satsuma decorator Kinkozan IV (Kobayashi Sobei, 1824-1884), along with Taizan Yohei, introduced gold overglaze enamel style decoration to Kyoto in the late nineteenth century. Their efforts proved very popular in the export market because of their very precise and detailed rendering. His descendants, including Kinkozan V (Kobayashi Sobei, 1868-1927), continued to use the Kinkozan name.

Satsuma saki set with tray, pot with lid, and six cups, all finely painted with floral and bird decoration by Kinkozan, pot 7.25" h., tray 8.25" l. Set $4,025-4,830

~ SATSUMA ~

Pair of Satsuma cups and saucers with handles from a set of nine, each with two panels decorated with groups of three men, decoration by Kinkozan, c. 1890. Set $5,800

~ 178 ~

~ SATSUMA ~

Tall Satsuma vase finely painted with two scenes of women in garden landscapes, decoration by Kinkozan, 11.75" h. $12,075

~ SATSUMA ~

Satsuma vase with three bands of painted decoration including wagons in flower blossoms for a summer festival, decoration by Kinkozan, c. 1890, 8.9" h. $4,025

~ 180 ~

~ SATSUMA ~

Top: Satsuma covered jar of globular shape with dark brown background and two reserves decorated with painted scenes of men and women in landscape settings, decoration by Kinkozan, c. 1890, 3.5" h. $2.575

Bottom Left & right: Round Satsuma dish with detailed painting of Japanese buildings and three men approaching, decoration by Kinkozan, c. 1890, 7.5" d. $3,220

~ SATSUMA ~

Satsuma vase with blue background and shaped reserves with figures in landscapes, decoration by Kinkozan, c. 1890, 9" h. $5,635

~ SATSUMA ~

Satsuma bulbous vase with reserves painted with groups of people in landscapes, decoration by Kinkozan with silver foil laid on, 5.75" h. $4,025-4,830

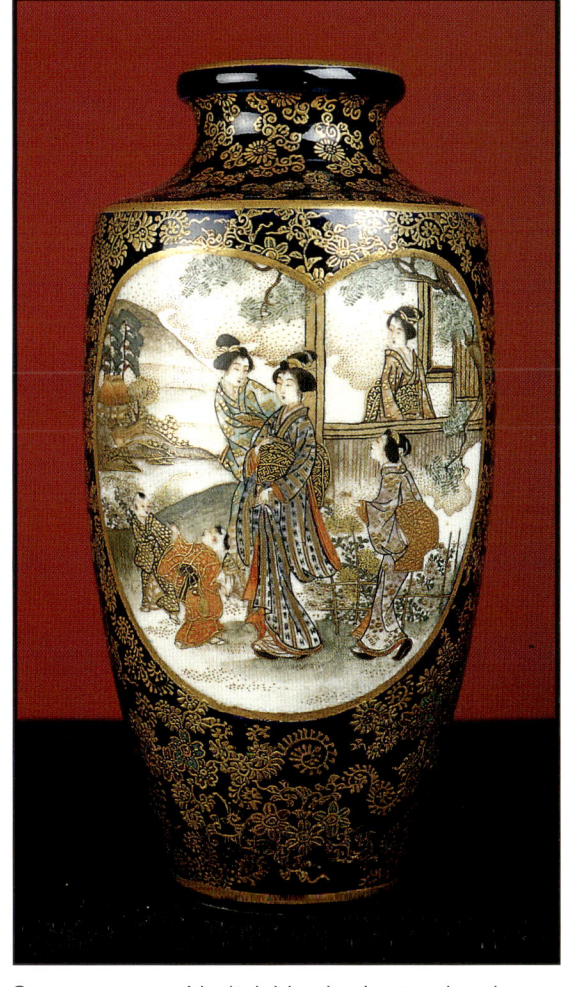

Satsuma vase with dark blue background and two reserves with women in a landscape setting and assorted furniture, decoration finely painted by Kinkozan, c. 1890, 5.75" h. $2,576

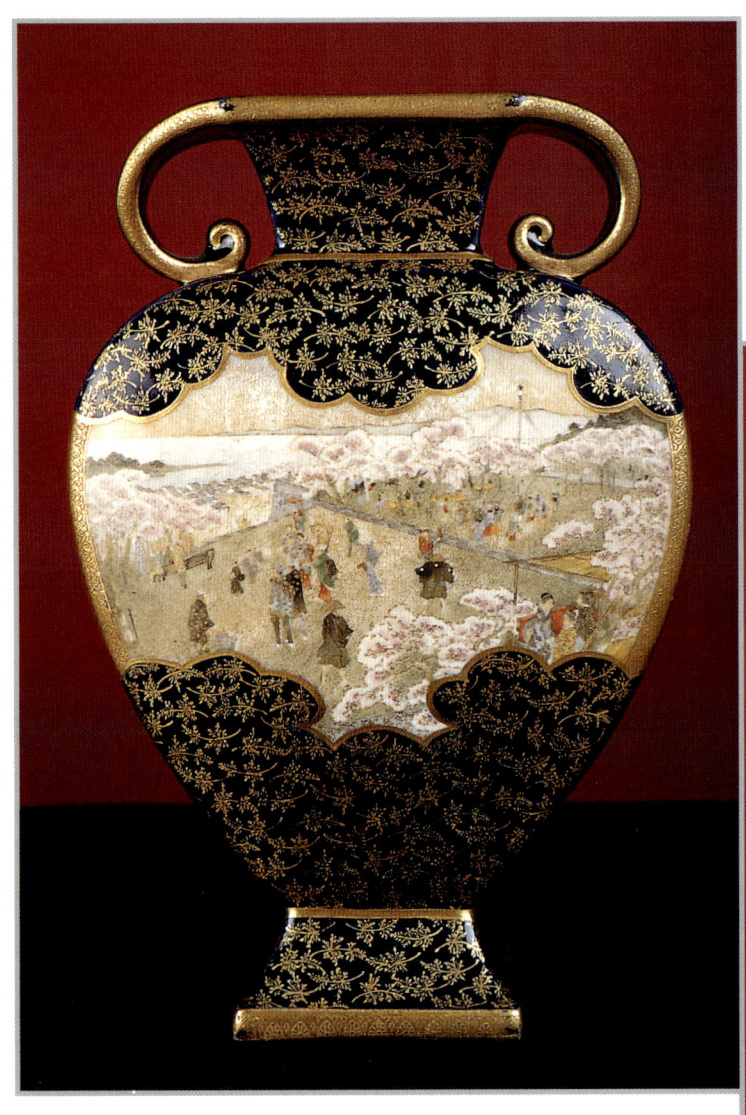

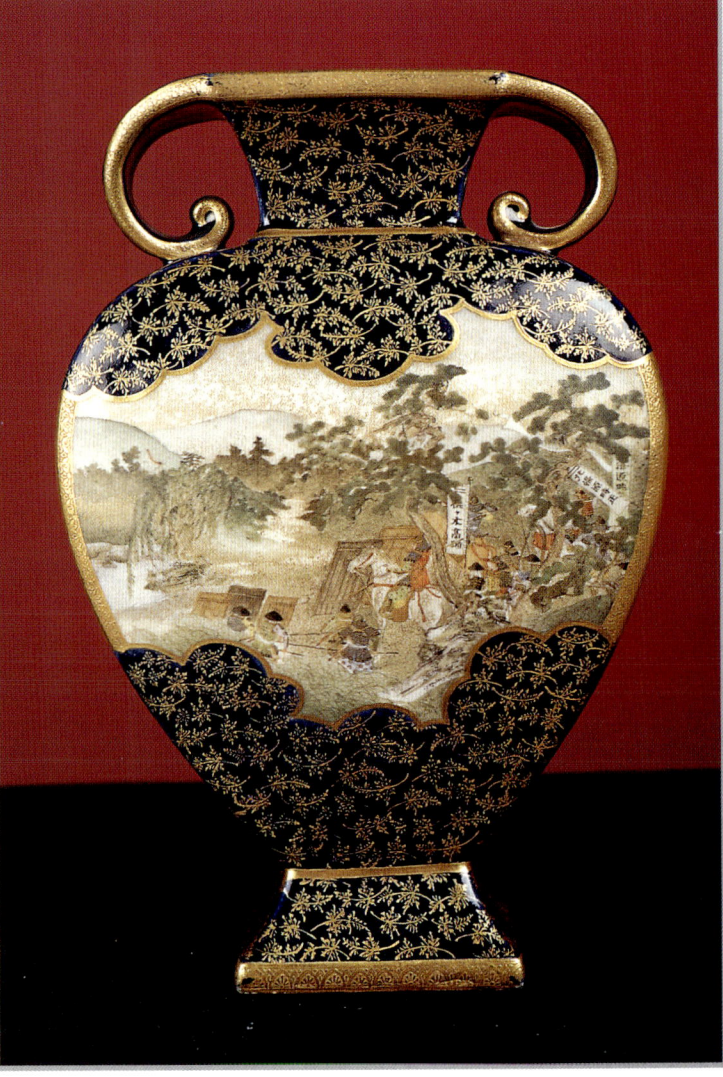

~ SATSUMA ~

Satsuma vase with square foot, rounded flat sides, and rectangular neck, with painted landscape scenes of a procession and two groups in landscape separated by a wall, decoration by Kinkozan, c. 1890, 6.6" h. $5,635

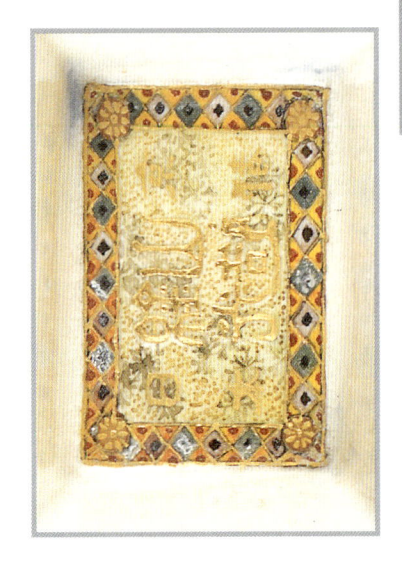

~ SATSUMA ~

Top: Satsuma *koro* with pastel painted floral decoration by Kinkozan, 8" h. $1,950

Bottom: Satsuma bowl decorated on the inside and outside with orange all-over floral blossoms, decoration by Kinkozan, c. 1890, 12.5" d. and 7.25" h. $4,830

~ 185 ~

~ SATSUMA ~

Tall Satsuma vase with landscape scenes in the reserves of the six sides, one showing women looking out from a building, decoration by Kinkozan, c. 1890, 18"h.

~ SATSUMA ~

~ 187 ~

~ SATSUMA ~

Fine Satsuma plate with painted decoration by Sozan of the Kinkozan workshop.

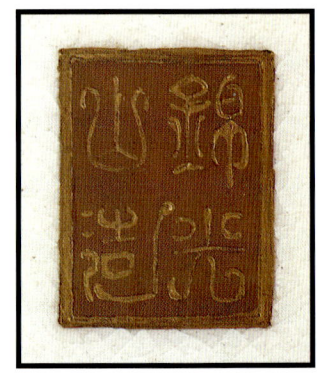

~ SATSUMA ~

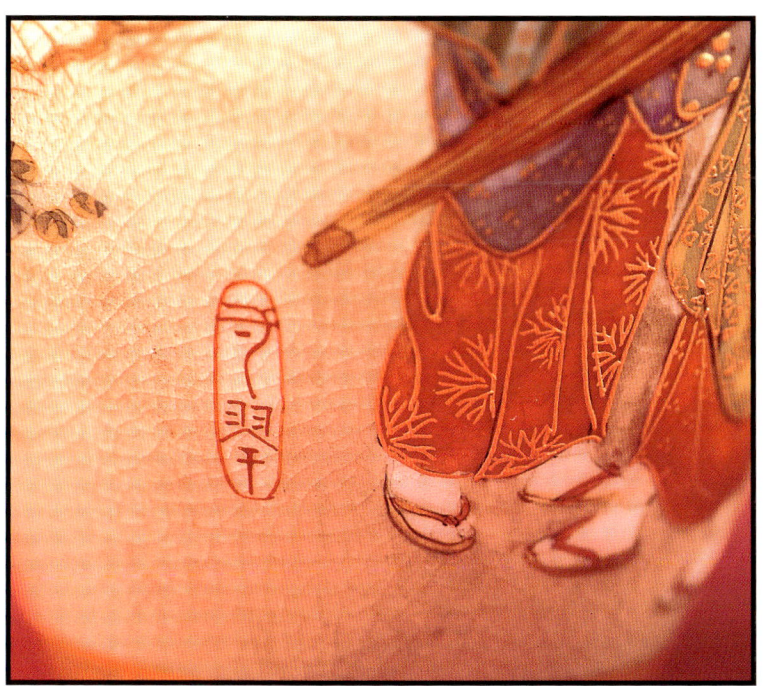

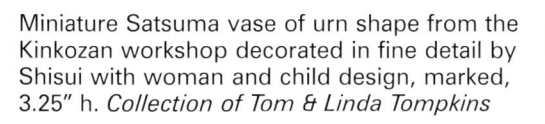

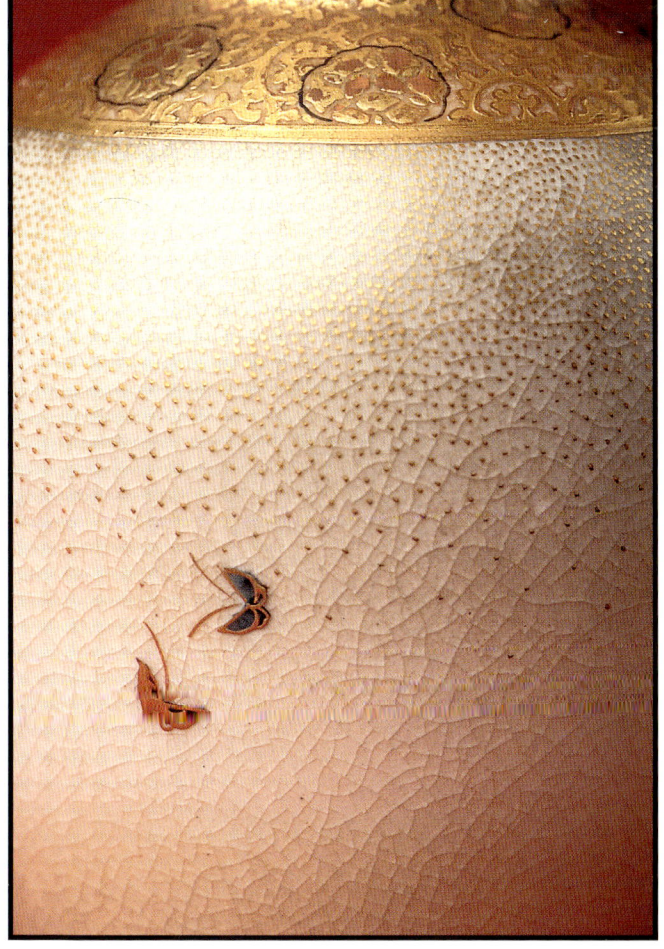

Miniature Satsuma vase of urn shape from the Kinkozan workshop decorated in fine detail by Shisui with woman and child design, marked, 3.25" h. *Collection of Tom & Linda Tompkins*

~ 189 ~

~ SATSUMA ~

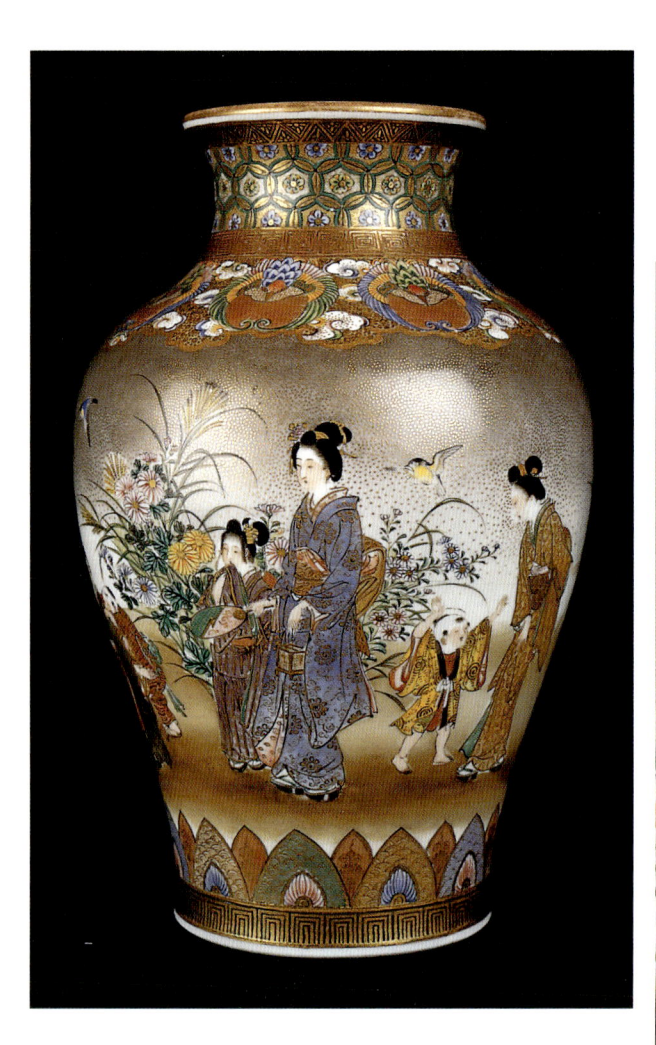

Satsuma vase painted with women and children in a garden setting, decoration by Kinkozan, c. 1890, 6.25" h.

Makuzu Kozan

This is perhaps the best known and most diverse potter/decorator of late nineteenth century Satsuma and studio porcelain wares. The son of the successful Miyagawa family of pottery makers in Kyoto, Miyagawa Toranosuke (1842-1916) used his artist name Miyagawa Kozan, or sometimes Makuzu Kozan. In the 1860s he made Satsuma style pottery from clay brought to Kyoto from Kagoshima in Satsuma province. In 1871 he moved to Ota near Yokohama to direct a kiln built specifically to produce ceramics for the export market. Here he made and oversaw production of various ceramic wares, some successfully recreating ancient styles. He also experimented with glazes and clay types to produce one-of-a kind studio ceramics. Between 1876 and 1915 his work was at most of the major International Exhibitions in Japan, America and Europe. In 1896 he was made a Member of the Japanese Imperial Household for Arts and Crafts.

Pair of large Satsuma double gourd vases with bases of four dark blue rounded panels and beige tops with scroll and leaf decoration, attributed to Makuzu Kozan, c. 1890, 13" h. $9,660

~ SATSUMA ~

Satsuma teapot in the form of a lion-headed bird, with Imperial decoration by Makuzu Kozan, c. 1885, 5.5" h. $6,440

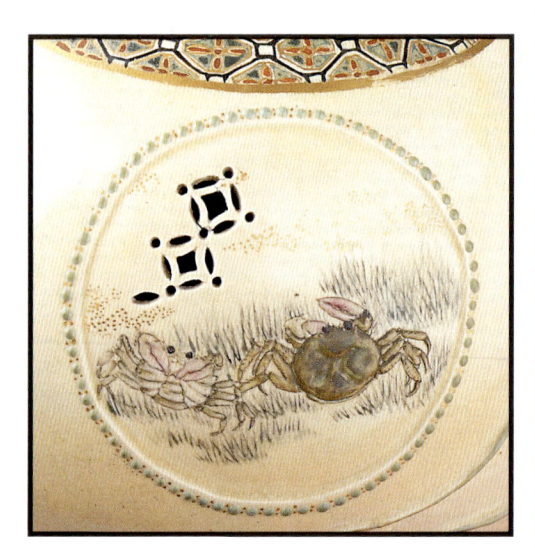

Large Satsuma covered bowl with pierced lid, four pierced side medallions, and relief green dragon decoration by Makuzu Kozan, c. 1885, 10.5" h. *Collection of Tom & Linda Tompkins*

~ SATSUMA ~

Studio pottery vase with green background with white wading cranes decoration, blue marks of Makuzu Kozan in a rectangle, c. 1910, 9" h. $4,025-4,830

Ryozan

Nishimura Zengoro (died 1841) was a celebrated tenth-generation potter in Kyoto who used the artist name Ryozan in the early nineteenth century. His work included Satsuma style pieces.

Ceramic artist Nakamura Tatsunosuke grew proficient under his predecessor's instruction and adopted the artist name Ryozan when he marked his exquisite late Satsuma style, decorated export pieces at Kyoto in the late nineteenth century. The work of both artists is of high quality.

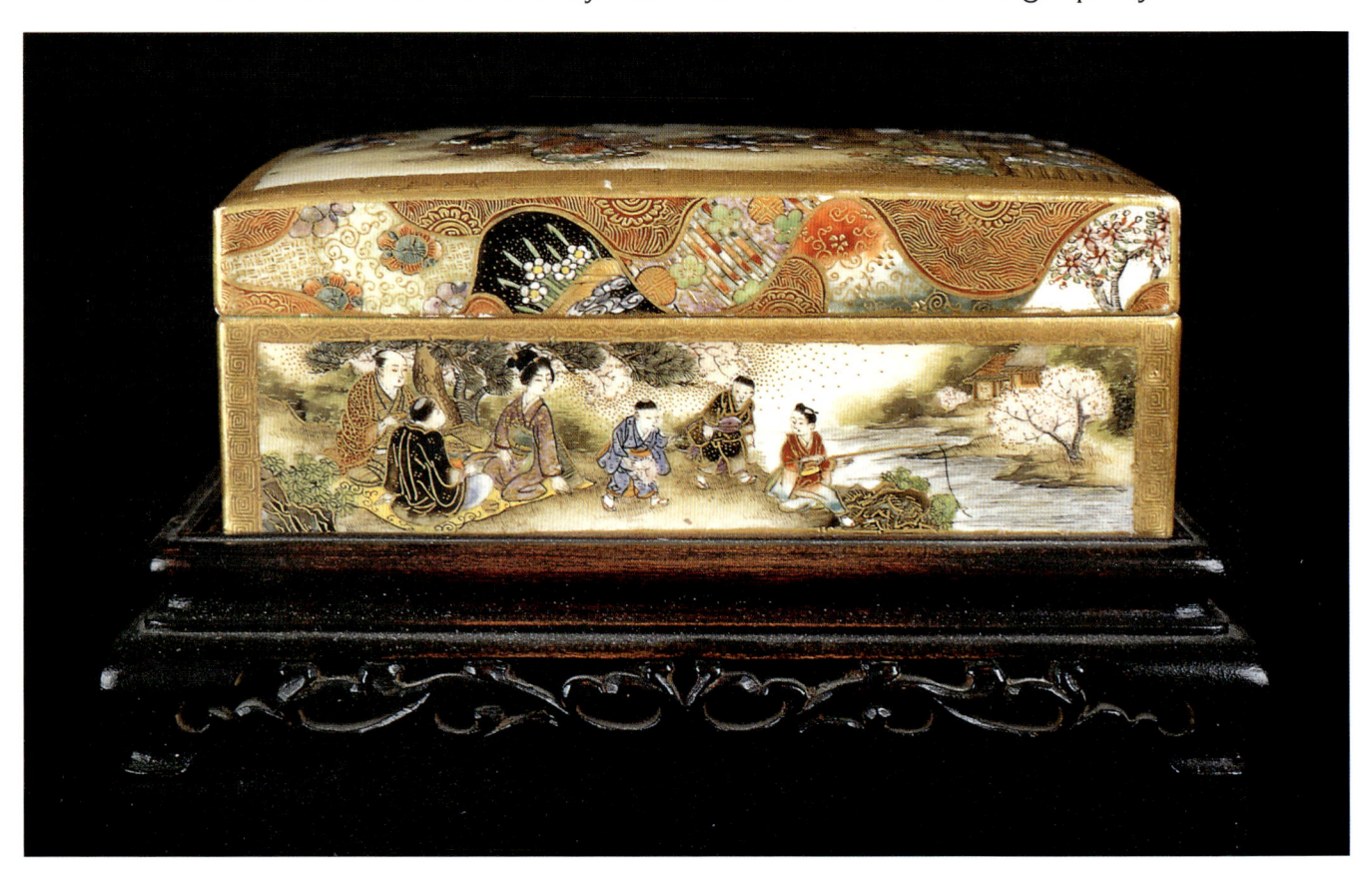

Rectangular Satsuma box with detailed painted decoration of people in landscapes, decoration by Ryozan, c. 1885, 5" long.

~ SATSUMA ~

Seikozan

The work of late nineteenth century Satsuma, export-style, decorator Seikozan is not frequently found today. It is invariably of very precise detail in soft and multiple colors with gold.

Pair of small Satsuma vases with flaring rims, a band of landscape decoration at the bases, people in cartouches at the body, and groups of people at the necks, decoration by Seikozan, c. 1885, 3.5" h.

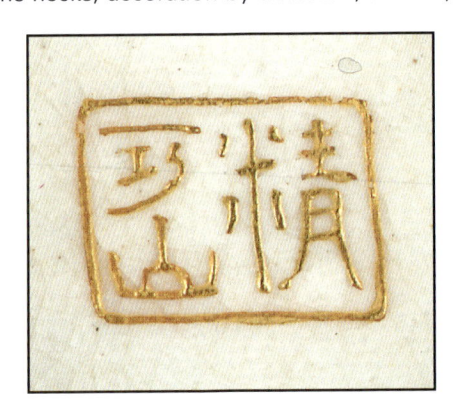

~ SATSUMA ~

Satsuma tea set of teapot, cream pitcher, covered sugar bowl, and three cups with handles and saucers, each piece with orange floral decoration by Seikozan, c. 1885.

~ SATSUMA ~

Set of five Satsuma plates with painted bird decoration by Seikozan, c. 1885, 7.5" d. Set $8,050

~ SATSUMA ~

Yabu Meizan

Satsuma style decorator Yabu Meizan (born Yabu Seishichi, 1853-1934), of Osaka, was the most proific producer of the detailed new "antique style" decorations on Satsuma ware in the late nineteenth and early twentieth centuries. He worked in Osaka from 1880 until 1916 with blanks from a kiln in Satsuma which he decorated for export dealers in Kyoto and Yokohama. From 1880 until c. 1890, he used primarily Chinese and Buddhist-derived themes as decorative devices, such as desciples of Buddha with golden halos (*rakan*) and groups of children playing games and participating in festivals (*karako*), which are called "hundred boys" decoration in the West. Then, about 1890, Yabu Meizan shifted to Japanese themes including samurai in combat and scenes inspired by Hiroshige's block print series of the Tokaido Road between Kyoto and Edo (Tokyo).

Between 1899 and 1910, Yabu Meizan represented Japan among the organizers of the exhibitions and traveled in official capacity to the International Exhibitions in the West. He produced and showed his Satsuma ceramics at Paris (1900), St. Louis (1904), and London (1910).

The detailed decorations on Yabu Meizan's Satsuma pieces utilized copper plate prints of the designs. "They were not used for paining directly to vases or plates, but they allowed the same outline design to be traced on paper an unlimited number of times and transferred to many different pieces." (Joe Earle, *Splendors of Meiji*, p. 118.) At the peak of his career, Yabu Meizan popularized decorations with thousands of butterflies or flowers and designs including long processions of people. He often placed his decorations inside intricately decoratd frames that ignored the shapes of the vessels. After 1910, his work declined in popularity as a general preference for Chinese arts developed in the West.

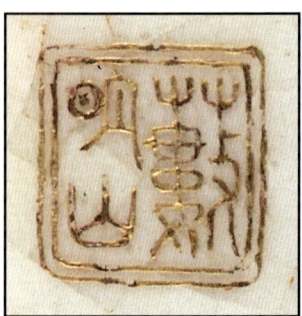

Two single and similar square vases with landscape decoration, one with diagonal stripes of butterflies and flowers in the base and the other with fan decorations in the base, decoration by Yabu Meizan, c. 1900, 5" h.

~ SATSUMA ~

Satsuma ovoid vase with a band at the base, painted as a chain of islands with fishing boats and net, and maple boughs at the neck, decoration by Yabu Meizan.

~ SATSUMA ~

Following three pages: Fine Satsuma bowl with painted decoration on the exterior of round medallions containing groups of people and frogs, the foot with monkeys, and the interior with a spiral band of foxes dressed as people in procession, decoration attributed to Yabu Meizan, c. 1890, 4.75" d. and 3.75" h.

~ SATSUMA ~

~ 203 ~

~ SATSUMA ~

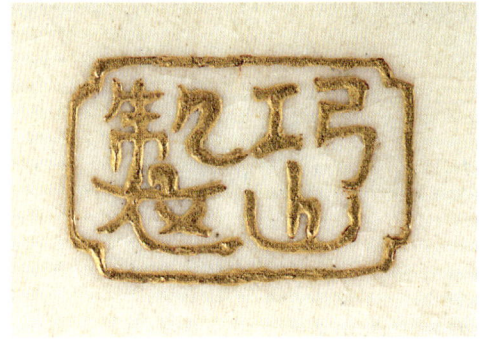

BIBLIOGRAPHY

Bushell, Stephen W. *Oriental Ceramic Art*. New York: Crown Publishers, Inc., 1980.

Cardero, c. Philip. *Hirado Ware*. Monterey: Art Asia Museum, 1989.

Christie's. *Important Japanese Works of Art from the Age of Western Influence*. London: Christie, Manson & Woods, Ltd.. 27 November, 1984.

Earle, Joe. *Splendors of Meiji, Treasures of Imperial Japan*, Masterpieces from the Khalili Collection. St. Petersburg, Florida: Broughton International Inc., 1999

Impey, Oliver R., *The Beginnings of the Export Trade in Japanese Porcelain*. Arita: The "Hyakunenan" Journal of Porcelain Study, No. 3., Summer, 1989.

Lawrence, Louis. *Satsuma, Masterpieces from the World's Important Collections*. London: Dauphin Publishing Limited, 1991.

Halén, Widar. *Christopher Dresser*. Oxford: Phaidon * Christies Limited, 1990.

Jenyns, Soame. *Japanese Porcelain*. London: Faber and Faber Limited, 1965.

Levy, Mervyn. *Libety Style, The Classic Years 1898-1910*. New York: Rizzoli International Publications, Inc., 1986.

Schiffer, Nancy N. *Imari, Satsuma and other Japanese Export Ceramics*. Atglen, Pennsylvania, Schiffer Publishing Ltd., 1997.

_____ *Japanese Porcelain 1800-1950*. Atglen, Pennsylvania, Schiffer Publishing Ltd., 1986.

Watson, Professor William, Ed. *The Great Japan Exhibition, Art of the Edo Period 1600-1868*. London: Royal Academy of Arts and Weidenfeld and Nicolson, 1981.

INDEX

Adams, William, 7
Anjiro, 6
Arita, 8
Arita ware, 14, 16
Ashenaga figure, 115
Augustus the Strong collection, 9

Banko ceramics, 11
Baralho, Crisobal, 6
Bungo, 6
Burghley Collection, 9

celadon, 30
Centennial Exhibition of 1876, 11
Charlottenberg collection, 9
Chicago, 11
Chinese Imari, 6, 7, 8
Company of Pure Water, 11
copper plate prints, 200

de Tories, Balthasar, 6
Deshima Island, 7, 8
Dresser, Christopher, 11
Dutch East India Company, 7-9, 14, 73

English East India Company, 7, 9
Enji Nishiura, 58

Fernandez, Joan, 6
Fillmore, President Millard, 9
Franks, Sir A. Woolaston, 11
Fukagawa Porcelain Manufacturing Company, 11
Fukagawa porcelain, 30, 36, 37, 40, 43, 46, 47, 56, 57, 61-63, 65, 70, 72, 79
Fukagawa, Chuji, 11
Funai, 6, 7

Gosu blue decoration, 129, 132, 134, 171

Hideyoshi, 8
Hirado Island, 6, 8
Hirado porcelain, 30, 73-86
Hiroshige block prints, 200
Hotei figurine, 75, 76, 90, 94, 114
hundred boys decoration, 200

Imari decoration, 6, 8-10, 11, 14-71
International Exhibitions, 11, 177, 191, 200
iron red background, 54
Izumiyama mountain, 8

Kagoshima province, 6, 191
Kagoshima, 107, 110, 111, 128, 131, 191
Kakiemon decoration, 8, 37
Kinkozan IV and V, 11, 129, 177-190
Kirutsu Kosho Kaisha Company, 11
Kobayashi Sobei, 177
Koransha porcelain, 11, 35, 36, 39, 50, 56, 57, 60, 64, 65, 70, 72
Kraak style dish, 7, 8
Kutani porcelain, 88-106
Kyoto, 6, 107, 177, 191, 194, 200

lamp, 24, 54, 151
Liberty, Arthur, 11
London, 11, 200
Loyola, Ignacius, 6

Macau, 6
Makuzu Kozan, 191-193
Miyagawa Kozan, 191
Miyagawa Toranosuke 191
Miyako, 6
Mt. Fuji decoration, 37
Myagawa Kozan, 11

Nabeshima decoration, 58
Nagasaki harbor, 7, 8
Nagato, 6
Nakamura Tatsunosuke, 92, 194
netsuke, 75
New York, 11
Nishimura Zengoro, 194

ormolu decoration, 9, 142, 145, 147
Osaka, 107, 200
Paris, 11, 70, 200
Pennsylvania Academy of Fine Arts, 11
Pennsylvania Museum and School of Industrial Art, 11
Perry, Commodore Matthew, 9
Philadelphia, 11
Pinto, Fernao Mendez, 6
Polo, Marco, 6

Raymond, Irving, 11
Ri Sampei, 8
Ryozan, 122, 194

Sakaida Kakiemon, 8
San Francisco, 11
Satsuma earthenware, 107-204
Sei Ji Kai Sha, 11
Seikozan, 196-199
Shimazu, 6
Shisui, 189
South Kensington Museum, 11
Sozan, 188
St. Louis, 11, 200
Sumida ceramics, 11

Taizan Yohei, 177
Tanegashima, 6
Tanzan, 126
tapestry decoration, 38, 41, 44, 133
Tenaga figure, 115
thousand faces decoration, 158, 161
Tiffany, Charles Louis, 11
Tiffany, Louis Comfort, 11
Tokaido Road, 200
Tokugawa Ieyasu, 7, 155
Tominiga Genroku, 58
Toyotomi Hideyoshi, 7

V. O. C., 8
Vantine, A. A. & Co., 11, 12, 13
Vereenigde Oost Indische Compagnie, 8
Victoria and Albert Museum, 11
Whistler, James McNeil, 11
Wilde, Oscar, 11

Xavier, Framcis, 6

Yabu Meizan, 11, 107, 200-204
Yabu Seishichi, 200
Yokohama, 11, 92, 107, 200

Zaimoto, Diego, 6
Zengoro Iraku, 126